Hopping into Literature and Primary Research

A Guide to Enhance Your Primary Literature Program

by
Laurie Chapin and Ellen Flegenheimer-Riggle

illustrated by Laurie Chapin

Cover by Jeff Van Kanegan

Copyright © Good Apple, 1992

Good Apple
1204 Buchanan Street, Box 299
Carthage, IL 62321-0299

S I M O N & S C H U S T E R *A Paramount Communications Company*

Copyright © Good Apple, 1992

ISBN No. 0-86653-661-2

Printing No. 9876543

Good Apple
1204 Buchanan Street, Box 299
Carthage, IL 62321-0299

Dedicated

with love to

Eleanor
Jim
Marge
and
Ernest . . .

who gave us our beginning

and
to baby Shelby

Special thanks to
Kimberly Cloud

GA1393

Table of Contents

Introduction

Hopping into Literature and Primary Research is a resource book that used distinguished children's literature as a vehicle to encourage higher level thinking, problem solving, creativity and research skills. Through lively discussion, creative activities and research experiences, children's learning in reading, language arts and other subject areas will be greatly enhanced. The ideas in the book provide a stimulus for the development of thoughts, experiences and creative ideas. It is especially relevant for those children showing high aptitude in these areas.

Hopping into Literature and Primary Research focuses on the development of activities which are based on two different theories that emphasize skills essential to the above average learner. These theories include the characteristics of creativity: fluency, flexibility, originality and elaboration, as well as Bloom's Taxonomy of Thinking Skills. Each activity is designed to challenge the children's abilities and encourage them to use those abilities to the fullest extent. The ideas will help children expand their minds by asking for new ideas and encourage the students to be independent problem solvers. The Primary Research activities will help the students develop lifelong learning skills including map reading, interviewing, library work, letter writing and observation.

Hopping into Literature and Primary Research provides concrete lessons and open-ended activities that teachers can use with an entire class, a small group or on an individual basis. The book should be used in a manner best suited to the needs of the teacher and the students. It is hoped that these ideas will serve as a springboard to other adventures in creativity and research as well as enrich the reading experiences of young readers.

May *Hopping into Literature and Primary Research* add magic and discovery to your literature program.

GA1393

Bloom's Taxonomy of Thinking Skills

Knowledge: questions that ask one to recall information
questions that check the basic facts

    Key Words: define, memorize, list, label, identify, show, recall, collect, recognize

Comprehension: questions that check one's understanding of the material

    Key Words: describe, explain, dramatize, retell, identify

Application: questions that ask one to apply and use information in a new situation

    Key Words: apply, experiment, show, solve, describe

Analysis: questions that ask one to break apart information and examine its separate parts and relationships

    Key Words: connect, relate, arrange, analyze, compare, contrast

Synthesis: questions that ask one to use information in a new, creative and original way

    Key Words: design, create, construct, imagine, suppose

Evaluation: questions that ask one to make judgments, with support, about the value of given information

    Key Words: judge, debate, decide, criticize

GA1393

Creative Thinking Activities

Fluency: activities that ask one to produce a large quantity of ideas or responses

Flexibility: activities that ask one to think of alternative ideas or categories of ideas and to change one's way of thinking about a given situation

Originality: activities that ask one to produce unique and novel ideas and responses

Elaboration: activities that ask one to expand upon a single idea by adding detail or making changes to make it more interesting and complete

GA1393

Hopping into Literature and Primary Research Will . . .

- enhance your primary literature or whole language program

- introduce students to distinguished children's literature

- introduce students to a variety of research materials

- enhance students' higher level thinking skills

- develop students' primary research skills

- encourage and expand students' creativity

- encourage students to look beyond the obvious

- promote a cooperative classroom environment

- involve students actively in the learning process

- provide the teacher with quality class discussion time

- provide the teacher with ideas for bulletin board displays

- provide the teacher with materials for the "already ready" student

- provide the teacher with learning center materials for independent study

GA1393

Suggestions for Using This Book

Bloom's Questions

- Select all or some of the questions and activities for a whole group discussion, small group or paired discussion or independent study.

- Create a comfortable atmosphere by accepting answers in a non-judgmental manner.

- Allow children ample time to respond to each question.

- Allow active participation from many children.

DESCRIBE A TIME WHEN YOUR PARENTS WERE PROUD OF YOU

1ST My first downhill ski race ribbon.

- Use blank shapes for making Bloom's Question cards. (See Blank Shape directions.)

- Use blank shapes for recording children's individual responses to Bloom's Questions.

GA1393

Creative Thinking Activities

- Be accepting of all answers.

- Allow adequate discussion time for brainstorming to become fruitful.

- Allow adequate "wait time" for each answer.

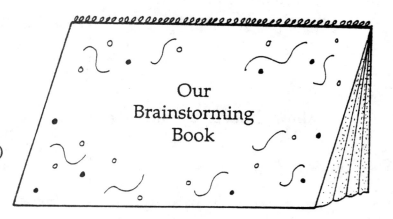

- Create a class "Brainstorming Book" to record fluency activities. (Use large lined chart paper. Glue wrapping paper on the front for a colorful cover.)

PAINTED THINGS . . .

road lines   graffiti
scenery   fingernails
walls   sweatshirts
masterpieces

- Use blank shapes for making Creative Thinking Activity cards. (See Blank Shape directions.)

- Use blank shapes for recording children's individual responses to Creative Thinking Activities.

GA1393

Blank Shapes

- Reproduce blank shapes to make shape cards. Print the questions and activities on them. Use one question per shape. Laminate and assemble cards on a ring.

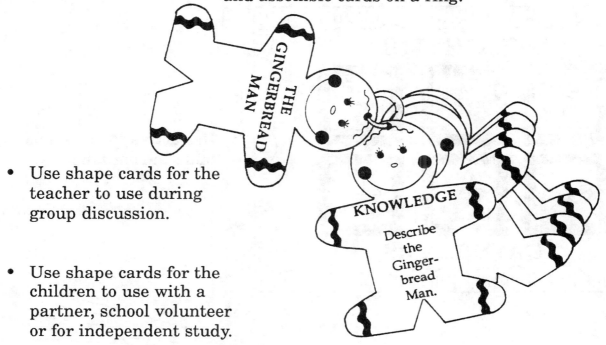

- Use shape cards for the teacher to use during group discussion.

- Use shape cards for the children to use with a partner, school volunteer or for independent study.

- Use shape cards at a learning center. Display them with the book and activity sheets.

- Use shapes for a class book or an individual student's book.

- Reproduce shapes for children to record individual thoughts.

- Use shapes to create a bulletin board display.

GA1393

Activity Sheets

- An asterisk designates written or illustrated activities that include activity sheets.

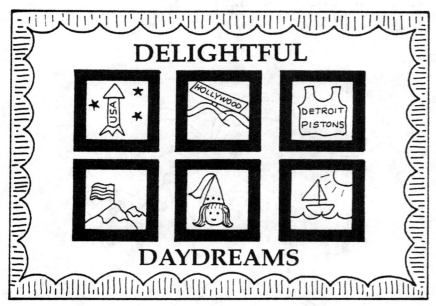

- Use activity sheets as a bulletin board display.

- Use activity sheets to create a class book.

- Assemble by laminating a colorful cover.

- Attach students' work with:
  - plastic spiral binding
  - hole punch with notebook ring or yarn
  - staple

Primary Research Center

The purpose of the Primary Research Center is to help students explore and investigate real people, places and things. It provides children with a purpose and motivation for using their reading skills. The center allows students to work individually or in small groups at their own pace. The center involves students actively in the learning process and enhances your whole language program.

The Primary Research Center should be in a designated area of your classroom. It may include:

activity sheets   crayons
direction cards   pencils
nonfiction books   colored pencils
glue   yarn
colored paper   paints
markers   paintbrushes
theme decorations

The Primary Research Center can most effectively be introduced by using the accompanying picture book story, discussion questions and activities. These will serve as a springboard to the research subject matter.

Each research activity should then be carefully explained and nonfiction books introduced.

1. Note that some research questions may require children to look outside of books and the classroom to find information. Parents, librarians and even the principal could be resources.

2. For younger children, try reading some nonfiction books to the whole class and research the questions together.

3. The teacher should share his/her expectations and rules for the use of the Primary Research Center.

4. Students should be encouraged to use their creative thinking skills to add unique and colorful details to their final research products.

The Primary Research Center provides a wonderful link to your classroom literature program. It should open many doors and avenues of exploration for your students.

 GA1393

Example of a Primary Research Center

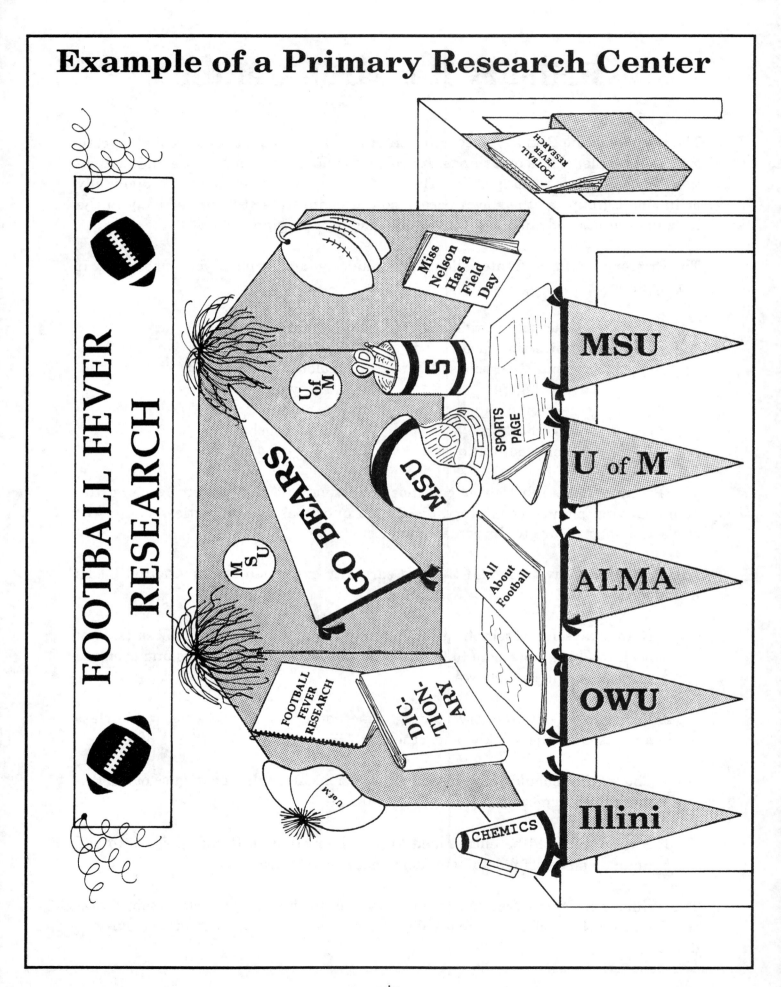

GA1393

BEDTIME FOR FRANCES

Russell Hoban
Scholastic, Inc., NY, 1960

Frances is having difficulty going to bed. She is convinced
a giant is in her room.

BLOOM'S QUESTIONS

KNOWLEDGE
   List three things Frances needed before she could go to sleep.

COMPREHENSION
   What made Frances finally fall asleep?

APPLICATION
   If you had difficulty falling asleep, what would you do to solve your problem?

ANALYSIS
   How is falling asleep at night different from waking up in the morning?

SYNTHESIS
   Write a letter from Frances to her best friend about her problems falling asleep.

EVALUATION
   Judge whether giving Frances a spanking for not falling asleep would be a good idea.
   Tell why or why not.

CREATIVE THINKING ACTIVITIES

FLUENCY
   Make a list of things that can help you fall asleep.

FLEXIBILITY
   Imagine that a giant was in Frances' bedroom. List the problems that Frances or
   the giant might encounter.

*ORIGINALITY
   Create a special object to help Frances fall asleep more easily. Make it one you
   would like to sleep with, too.

*ELABORATION
   Look closely at the last picture in the book. Frances' bedroom needs some decorations. Draw a picture to hang on her wall.

GA1393

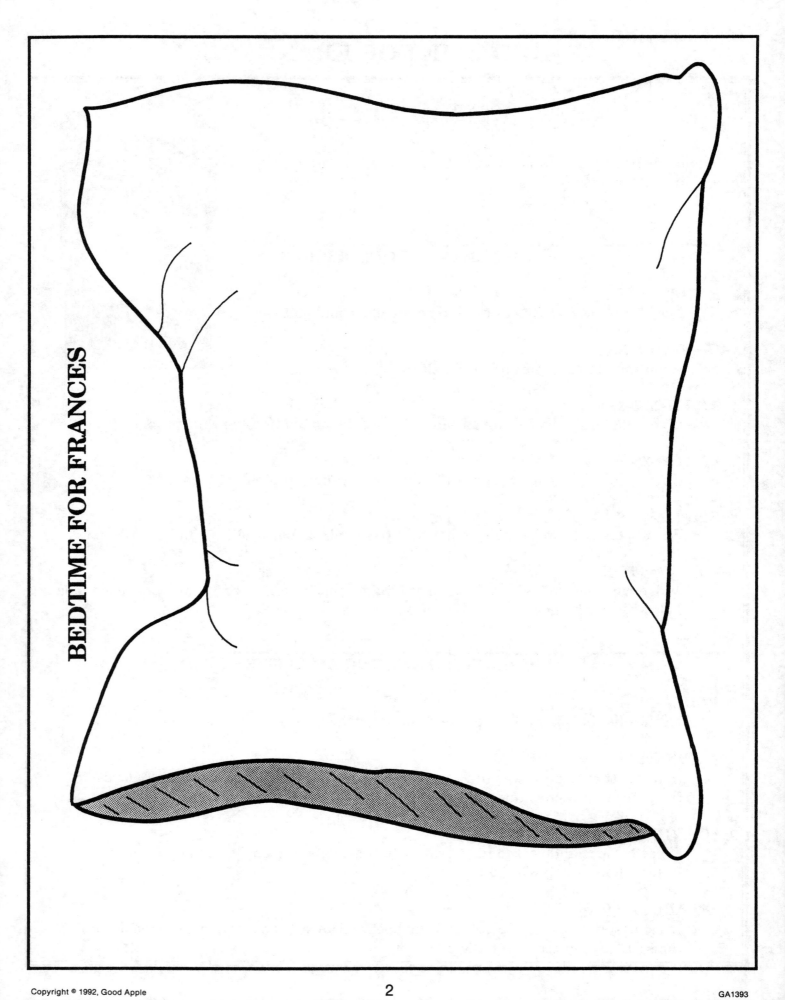

BEDTIME FOR FRANCES

2

Create a special object to help Frances
fall asleep more easily. Make it one you
would like to sleep with, too.

Peaceful Sleeper _____

GA1393

Sweet Dreams

Draw a picture to hang on the wall in
Frances' bedroom. Make it one that
will help her have sweet dreams.

Sweet Dreamer _____

GA1393

BEDTIME AND ME RESEARCH

Research Project

- ✦ Students will use their own experiences as a resource guide.
- ✦ Students will create a Bedtime and Me Mobile.

Research Center

- ✦ The Bedtime and Me Research Center should include:

  - a special place in your classroom decorated with a bedtime/nighttime motif including a blanket, night-light, stuffed animals and lullaby books.
  - fiction books related to bedtime rituals.
  - a laminated copy of the student activity packet (for teacher use and display at the center).

- ✦ Provide each student with a copy of the circle research shapes including the cover and student directions.

- ✦ The completed research project can be displayed as a mobile hanging from the ceiling of your classroom or over the research center; or students may want to take their mobiles home to hang in their bedrooms.

- ✦ Award each student an Expert Certificate upon completion of the center.

Research Resources

- ✦ Berger, Barbara Helen. *Grandfather Twilight.* New York: Philomel, 1984.

- ✦ Brown, Margaret Wise. *Goodnight Moon.* New York: Harper & Row, 1947.

- ✦ Ginsberg, Mirra. *Where Does the Sun Go at Night?* New York: Greenwillow, 1980.

- ✦ Wood, Audrey. *The Napping House.* New York: Harcourt Brace, 1984.

- ✦ Ziefert, Harriet. *I Won't Go to Bed!* New York: Little, Brown, 1987.

GA1393

BEDTIME AND ME RESEARCH

GA1393

Discuss your bedtime rituals with your family. Write your name and draw a picture of your face in the first circle. Then complete all of the sentences on the circles. Color pictures to add interest to each circle.

When you are finished, cut out the circles and lay them in a long, vertical row with your face at the top. Tie them together with yarn. You now have a Bedtime and Me hanging!

7

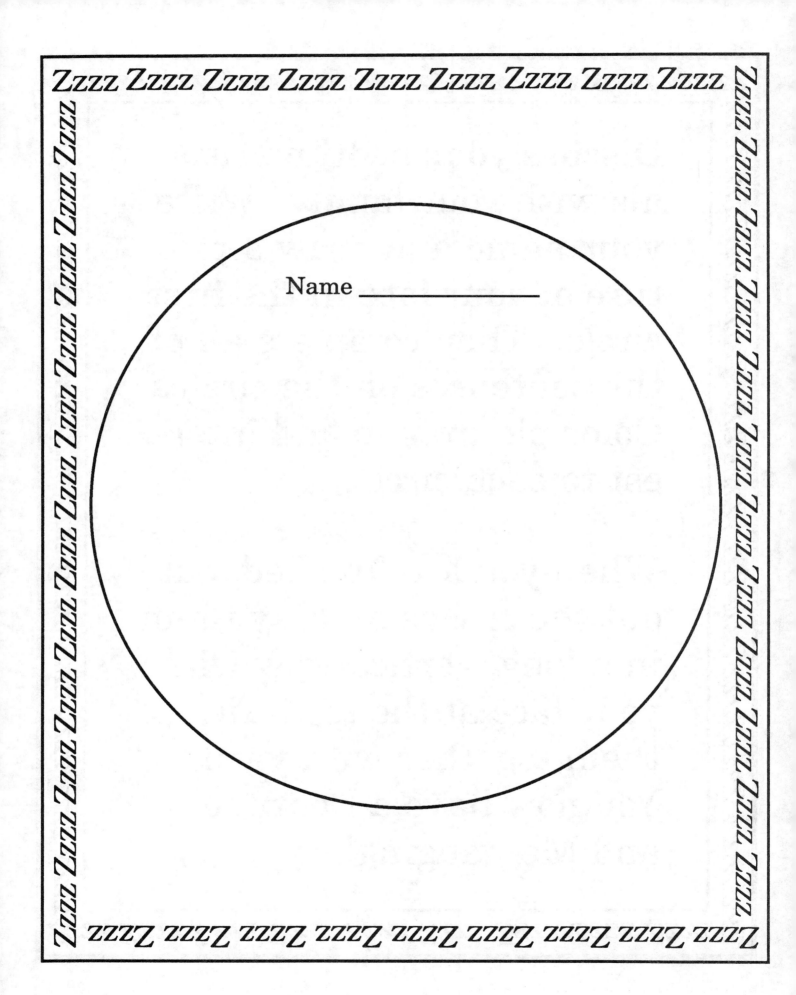

Name _____

8

GA1393

My bedroom looks like this . . .

Zzzz Zzzz Zzzz Zzzz Zzzz Zzzz Zzzz Zzzz Zzzz

I go to bed at _____ o'clock
on most nights . . .

Zzzz Zzzz Zzzz Zzzz Zzzz Zzzz Zzzz Zzzz Zzzz

My favorite thing to
sleep with is . . .

GA1393

Zzzz Zzzz Zzzz Zzzz Zzzz Zzzz Zzzz Zzzz Zzzz

If I could change one
thing about my bedtime
it would be . . .

Zzzz Zzzz Zzzz Zzzz Zzzz Zzzz Zzzz Zzzz Zzzz

12

Zzzz Zzzz Zzzz Zzzz Zzzz Zzzz Zzzz Zzzz Zzzz

My favorite bedtime
story is . . .

GA1393

BEDTIME AND

ME EXPERT

has explored and investigated the topic of Bedtime. Congratulations on your newly learned knowledge!

Teacher _____

Date _____

GA1393

THE BIGGEST BEAR

Lynd Ward
Houghton Mifflin Co., Boston, 1952

Johnny Orchard and the Biggest Bear share many adventures in this book.

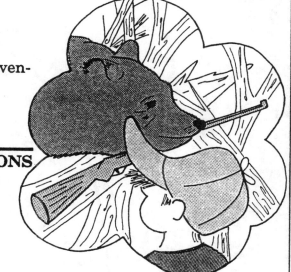

BLOOM'S QUESTIONS

KNOWLEDGE
List the foods the bear liked to eat in the story.

COMPREHENSION
Why did the bear keep returning to Johnny?

APPLICATION
Try to imagine what you would do if the bear kept returning.

ANALYSIS
Compare a bear's life in the forest with a bear's life in a zoo.

SYNTHESIS
Share a new way for Johnny to return the bear to the forest.

EVALUATION
Was it a good idea to take the bear to the zoo? Tell why or why not.

CREATIVE THINKING ACTIVITIES

FLUENCY
Brainstorm a list of all the kinds or names of bears you can think of.

FLEXIBILITY
Categorize your list of bears into real and make-believe.

ORIGINALITY
Write a letter to the zookeeper from Johnny telling him how to take care of the biggest bear.

ELABORATION
Elaborate on the Biggest Bear's cage at the zoo. Create a large sign and decorations to hang on the cage.

GA1393

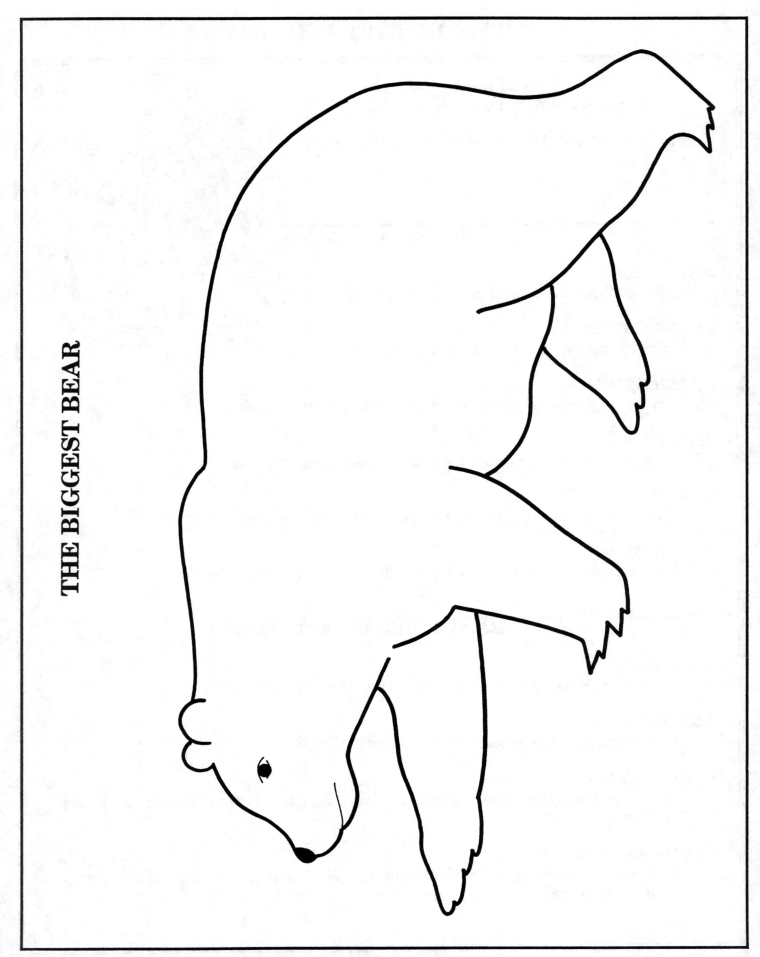

THE BIGGEST BEAR

16

Write a letter to the zookeeper from Johnny telling him
how to take care of the biggest bear.

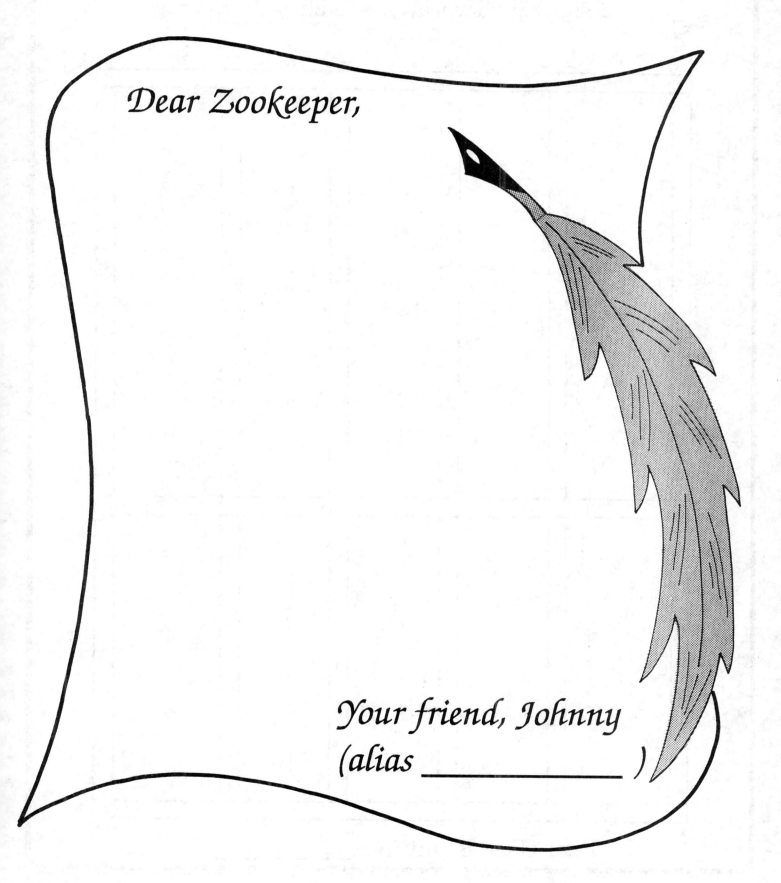

Dear Zookeeper,

Your friend, Johnny
(alias _____)

17

GA1393

Elaborate on the Biggest Bear's cage at the zoo. Create a sign and decorations to hang on the cage.

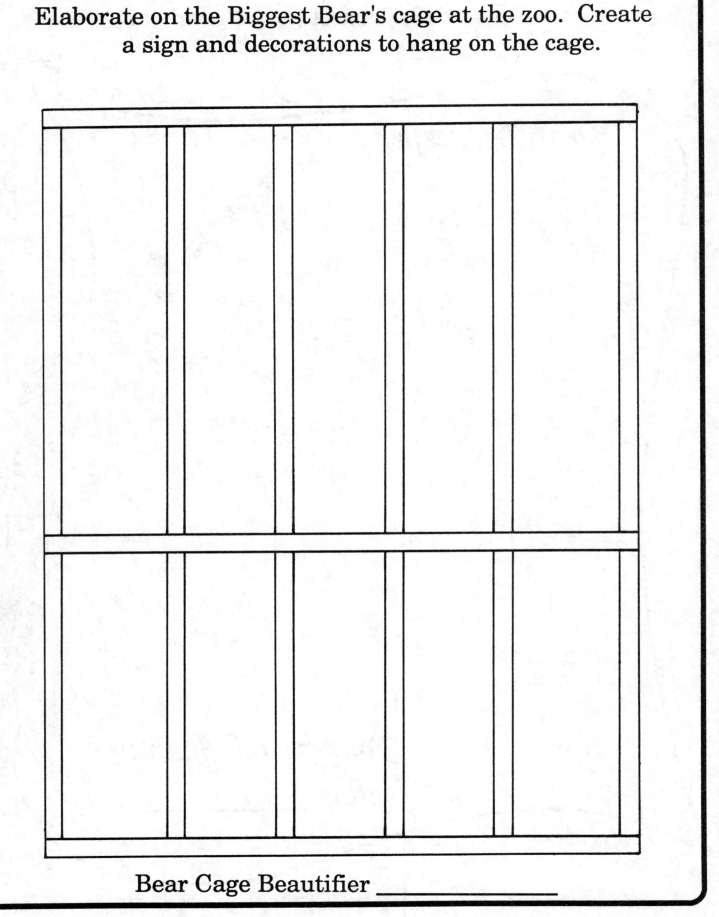

Bear Cage Beautifier _____

GA1393

BEAR FACTS RESEARCH

Research Project

✦ Students will research six bear facts.
✦ Students will create a bear mobile.

Research Center

✦ The Bear Facts Research Center should include:

- a special place in your classroom decorated with a bear theme including bear products such as stuffed animals, hats, slippers or T-shirts.
- bear research resources.
- a laminated copy of the student activity packet (for teacher use and display at the center).

✦ Provide each student with a set of bear shapes, including the cover and student directions.

✦ The completed research projects can be displayed as a bulletin board, or set up as a mobile by tying yarn to the bears and hanging them from hangers, small tree branches or thin dowels.

✦ Award each student an Expert Certificate upon completion of the center.

Research Resources

✦ Johnston, Ginny, and Judy Cutchins. *Andy Bear*. New York: William Morrow & Co., 1985.

✦ Patent, Dorothy Hinshaw. *The Way of the Grizzly*. New York: Clarion, 1987.

✦ Schlein, Miriam. *Pandas*. New York: MacMillan Publishing, 1989.

✦ Weaver, John L. *Grizzly Bears*. New York: Dodd, 1982.

✦ Wexo, John Bonnett. *Bears*. New York: Wildlife, 1982.

GA1393

BEAR FACTS RESEARCH

GA1393

Write the title, BEAR FACTS, and your name on the first bear shape. Then complete each "bear fact."

When you are finished, cut out each bear, decorate, and assemble as a mobile or book.

21

GA1393

Name _____

22

A large city in the United States has a football and baseball team named after bears. Ask a sports enthusiast to get your answer.

23

GA1393

Write the name of the bear who is famous for fighting forest fires.

24

GA1393

A special kind of bear
comes from China and eats
bamboo. Who is it?

25

List the names
of three famous
storybook bears.

26

GA1393

Visit a local store and find the names of three companies that make teddy bears.

27

GA1393

The teddy bear is named
after an American president.
Can you discover
who it is?

28

GA1393

Name a bear that can be
found on T V.

29

GA1393

BEAR EXPERT

_____ has explored and investigated the topic of Bears. Congratulations on your newly learned knowledge!

Teacher _____

Date _____

30

THE BIG ORANGE SPLOT

Daniel Manus Pinkwater
Scholastic, Inc., NY, 1977

Mr. Plumbean painted his house and the neighbor's couldn't believe their eyes. They thought Mr. Plumbean had gone crazy.

BLOOM'S QUESTIONS

KNOWLEDGE
   Describe Mr. Plumbean's house after he painted it.

COMPREHENSION
   What did people mean when they said, "Plumbean has popped his cork, flipped his wig, blown his stack and dropped his stopper?"

APPLICATION
   Describe one "crazy" thing you have done in your own life.

ANALYSIS
   Compare Mr. Plumbean's house with your own house.

SYNTHESIS
   Design a house that fits your dreams.

EVALUATION
   Decide whether it was a good idea for Mr. Plumbean to change his house.

CREATIVE THINKING ACTIVITIES

FLUENCY
   Brainstorm things that are painted.

FLEXIBILITY
   Look at your list of painted things. Divide them into two categories: Spray-painted items and hand-painted items.

ORIGINALITY
   Turn the "big orange splot" into something other than a part of Mr. Plumbean's house.

ELABORATION
   Mr. Plumbean's street is missing appropriate landscaping. Choose one of the houses and add as many unusual flowers, bushes and trees as you can.

GA1393

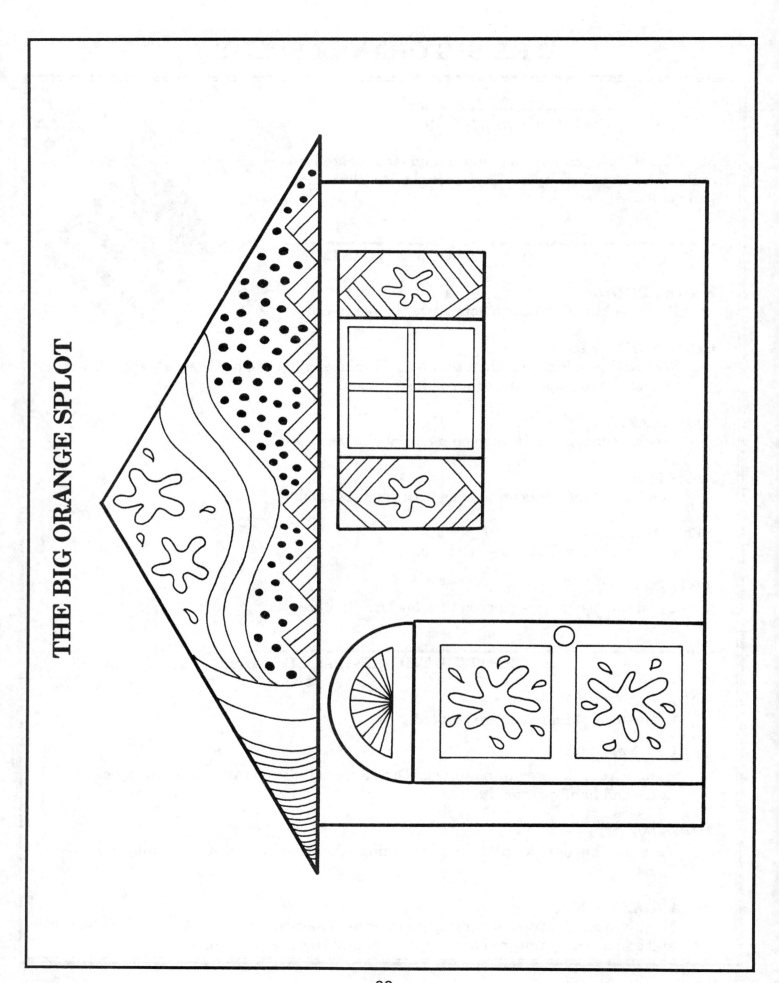

THE BIG ORANGE SPLOT

GA1393

Turn the "big orange splot" into something other than a part of Mr. Plumbean's house.

Creative Thinker _____

GA1393

Add unusual landscaping to one of
the houses on Mr. Plumbean's street.

Landscape Architect _____

HOUSE DETECTIVE RESEARCH

Research Project

+ Students will use their own homes as their resource guides.
+ Students will complete the house detective questionnaire.

Research Center

+ The House Detective Research Center should include:

  - a special place in your classroom decorated with a theme related to housing including items such as a doll house, blueprints or architects' tools.
  - house and home research resources.
  - a laminated copy of the student activity packet (for teacher use and display at the center).

+ Provide each student with a copy of the house detective questionnaire including the cover and student directions.

+ The completed research project can be displayed in a classroom book. Select a student to make a cover. Title your book *Investigating Our Houses*.

+ Award each student an Expert Certificate upon completion of the center.

Research Resources

+ D'Alelio, Jane. *I Know That Building!* Washington, D.C.: The Preservation Press, 1989.

+ Devlin, Harry. *To Grandfather's House We Go.* New York: Parents Magazine Press, 1969.

+ Devlin, Harry. *What Kind of House Is That?* New York: Parents Magazine, 1969.

+ Isaacson, Philip M. *Round Buildings, Square Buildings & Buildings That Wiggle Like a Fish.* New York: Alfred A. Knopf, 1988.

+ LeSieg, Theo. *Come Over to My House.* New York: Random House, 1966.

GA1393

HOUSE
DETECTIVE
RESEARCH

GA1393

Be a house detective and investigate your own home. Observe closely the inside and outside of your home. Then complete the letter about your house. Mail it to a friend who has never seen your house.

HOME SWEET HOME

_______________ (date)

Dear _______________,

My house is made of _________, _________, _________ and _________. It is called a _________________ house. It is located on ___________________ and its dominant color is __________. It has __________ windows in the front and _______ doors. The color of my front door is __________. The most unique feature on the exterior of the house is ______________________________.

Inside my house, there are _______ rooms. My favorite room is ____________________.

I like it best because ____________________

____

____

My favorite possession in my house is ____________. My least favorite thing

HOME SWEET HOME

about my house is _____ because

_____

_____

_____.

My bedroom is located _____
_____ in my house. The walls are
_____; the carpet is _____. The colors
in my room are _____, _____,
_____, _____ and _____. I
have _____ hangings on
the wall. There are _____ pieces of
furniture in my bedroom. I must clean my
room _____ times a week.

I hope you can visit my house someday.
Please write and tell me about your house.

_____,

_____

P.S. I've enclosed a picture of my house
and my favorite room in it.

GA1393

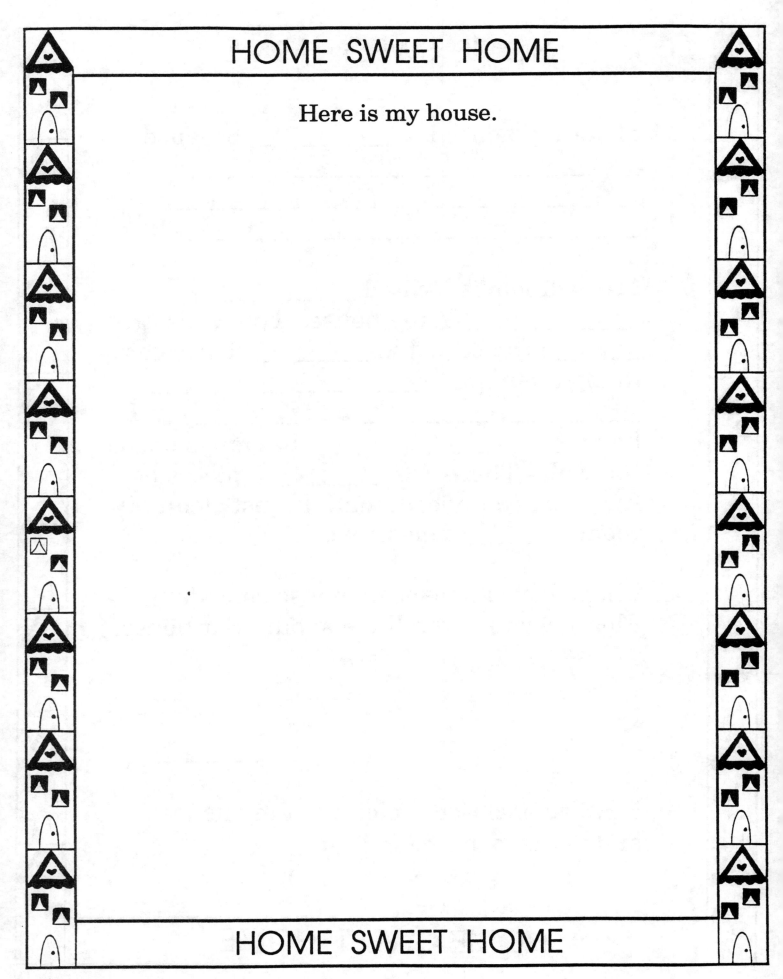

HOME SWEET HOME

Here is my house.

HOME SWEET HOME

GA1393

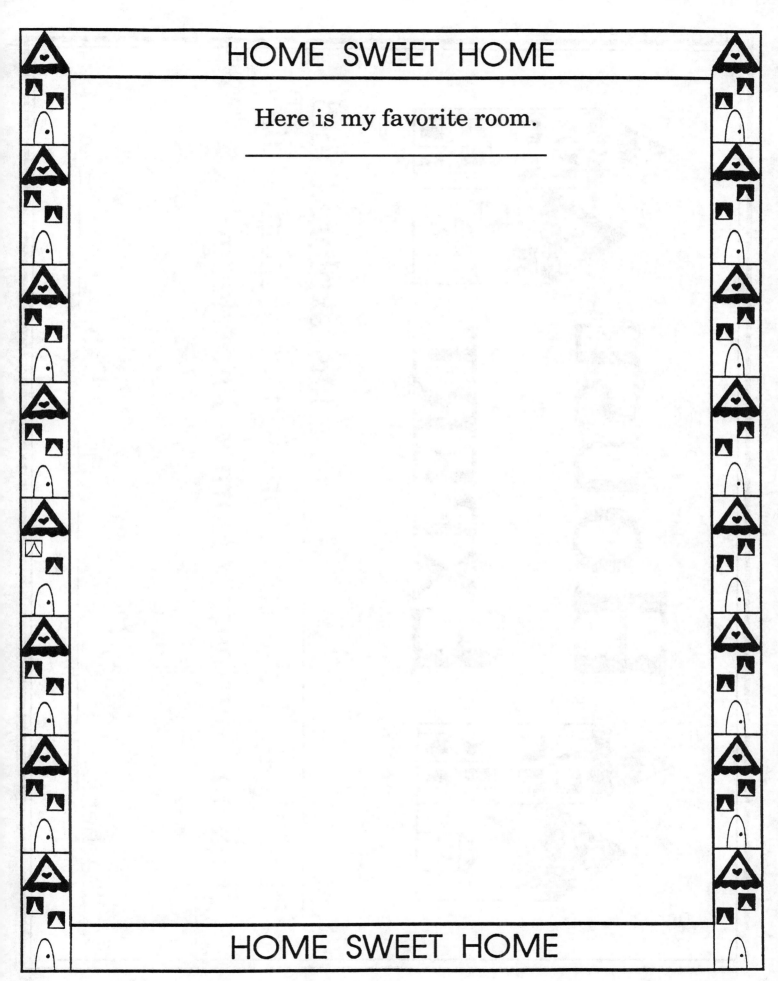

Here is my favorite room.

_____

HOME SWEET HOME

41

GA1393

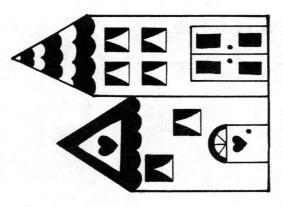

HOUSE EXPERT

_____ has explored and investigated the topic of Houses. Congratulations on your newly learned knowledge!

Teacher _____

Date _____

42

THE GINGERBREAD MAN

Scholastic, Inc., NY, 1967

A gingerbread boy escapes from the oven and runs from everyone except the fox.

BLOOM'S QUESTIONS

KNOWLEDGE
Describe the gingerbread boy.

COMPREHENSION
Explain how the gingerbread boy escaped from the oven.

APPLICATION
Share an experience about baking cookies from your own life.

ANALYSIS
List and analyze what is real and make-believe in the story.

*SYNTHESIS
Design a new cookie to escape from the old woman's oven. Give it a name and lots of decorations.

EVALUATION
Evaluate the words the gingerbread boy calls to everyone.

CREATIVE THINKING ACTIVITIES

FLUENCY
The gingerbread boy is made with an ingredient called *ginger*. Brainstorm a long list of spices. (You may need to check your kitchen or grocery store.)

FLEXIBILITY
Divide your list of spices into as many categories as you can: colors, texture, taste, smell, etc.

*ORIGINALITY
Create a new chant for the gingerbread boy to say as he runs away from everyone.

ELABORATION
Add a gingerbread family to the gingerbread boy. Decorate and name each member of his family.

GA1393

THE GINGERBREAD BOY

44

Design a new cookie to escape from the old woman's oven. Give it a name and lots of decorations.

Cookie Maker _____

45

GA1393

Create a new chant for the gingerbread
boy to say as he runs away from
everyone he meets.

Script Writer _____

46

GA1393

COOKIES AND COOKBOOK RESEARCH

Research Project

- ✦ Students will use cookbooks as their research guide.
- ✦ Students will complete the cookbook questionaire.

Research Center

- ✦ The Cookies and Cookbook Research Center should include:

  - a special place in your classroom decorated with a cookie theme including cookie cutters, baking equipment, utensils and a variety of cookie packages.
  - cookbook research resources.
  - a laminated copy of the student activity packet (for teacher use and display at the center).

- ✦ Provide each student with a copy of the cookies and cookbook questionaire including the cover and student directions.

- ✦ The completed research projects can be displayed.

- ✦ Award each student an Expert Certificate upon completion of the center.

Research Resources

- ✦ *Betty Crocker's New Boys & Girls Cookbook*. New York: Prentice Hall Press, 1990.

- ✦ Coyle, Rena. *My Very First Cookbook*. New York: Workman Publishing, 1985.

- ✦ Kedna, Margaret, and Phillis S. Williams. *Cooking Wizardry for Kids*. New York: Barron's, 1990.

- ✦ Linton, Marilyn. *Just Desserts*. New York: Kids Can, 1986.

- ✦ Wilkes, Angela. *My First Cookbook*. New York: Alfred A. Knopf, 1989.

GA1393

COOKIES
AND
COOKBOOK
RESEARCH

GA1393

Select a cookbook.

Use the index to find
cookie recipes and other
cookie-making informa-
tion.

Complete the activity
pages using the cook-
book as your research
guide.

49

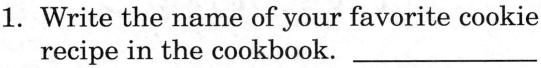

1. Write the name of your favorite cookie recipe in the cookbook. _____
   _____

2. How many ingredients are listed in your recipe? _____

3. How many cookies does your recipe say it will make? _____
   Is that number more or less than one dozen? _____

4. List at least three pieces of cooking equipment required to complete your recipe. _____

5. At what temperature should the oven be set to bake your cookies? _____

6. If you could taste one ingredient in the cookie recipe, what would it be?

   _____

7. Estimate how long it would take you to make your cookies from start to finish. _____

8. List two rules for baking cookies. ___

   _____

   _____

9. If you could share your cookies with someone, who would it be? _____

10. Are all cookies round? _____
    How can you prove your answer? _____

    _____

11. Name a cookie recipe in the cookbook that you would like to try. Tell why.

    _____

    _____

12. Name a cookie recipe in the cookbook that you would *not* like to try. Tell why. _____

    _____

GA1393

Compare Two Cookie Recipes

Recipe #1 _____   Recipe #2 _____

Which makes more cookies? _____

_____

Which uses more eggs? _____

_____

Which uses more flour? _____

_____

Which uses less sugar? _____

_____

Which requires fewer steps? _____

_____

Which requires the hottest oven? _____

_____

Which will bake longer? _____

_____

Cookie Recipe Hunt

Find and name a recipe that requires:

a greased cookie sheet _____

rolling the dough _____

a liquid ingredient _____

1 egg _____

1 cup sugar _____

powdered sugar _____

brown sugar _____

stirring and beating _____

nuts _____

candy _____

frosting _____

a spice _____

baking longer than 10 minutes _____

makes over 24 cookies _____

you serve on a holiday _____

COOKBOOK EXPERT

_____ has explored and investigated the topic of Cookbooks. Congratulations on your newly learned knowledge!

Teacher _____

Date _____

54

THE GROUCHY LADYBUG

Eric Carle
Thomas Y. Crowell, NY, 1977

The Grouchy Ladybug is always looking for someone to fight. He bullies everyone from sunrise to sunset, until he finally meets his match.

BLOOM'S QUESTIONS

KNOWLEDGE
List all the animals in the story.

COMPREHENSION
Why does the ladybug always say, "Oh, you're not big enough," and then fly off?

APPLICATION
How would you feel if someone bullied you? What would you do?

ANALYSIS
Compare the ladybug to the whale. How are they the same? How are they different?

SYNTHESIS
Imagine what would have happened if the ladybug and the skunk had become involved in a fight. Share your ideas with a small group.

EVALUATION
Judge whether you would like to be the ladybug's friend.

CREATIVE THINKING ACTIVITIES

FLUENCY
Make a list of as many insects as you can.

FLEXIBILITY
Select five to ten insects from your list and rank order them from favorite to least favorite.

*ORIGINALITY
Design a one-of-a-kind insect. Color or paint a picture of it. Create an unusual name for it.

*ELABORATION
Write and then role-play a conversation between the Grouchy Ladybug and the Friendly Ladybug after they wake up the next morning.

GA1393

THE GROUCHY LADYBUG

56

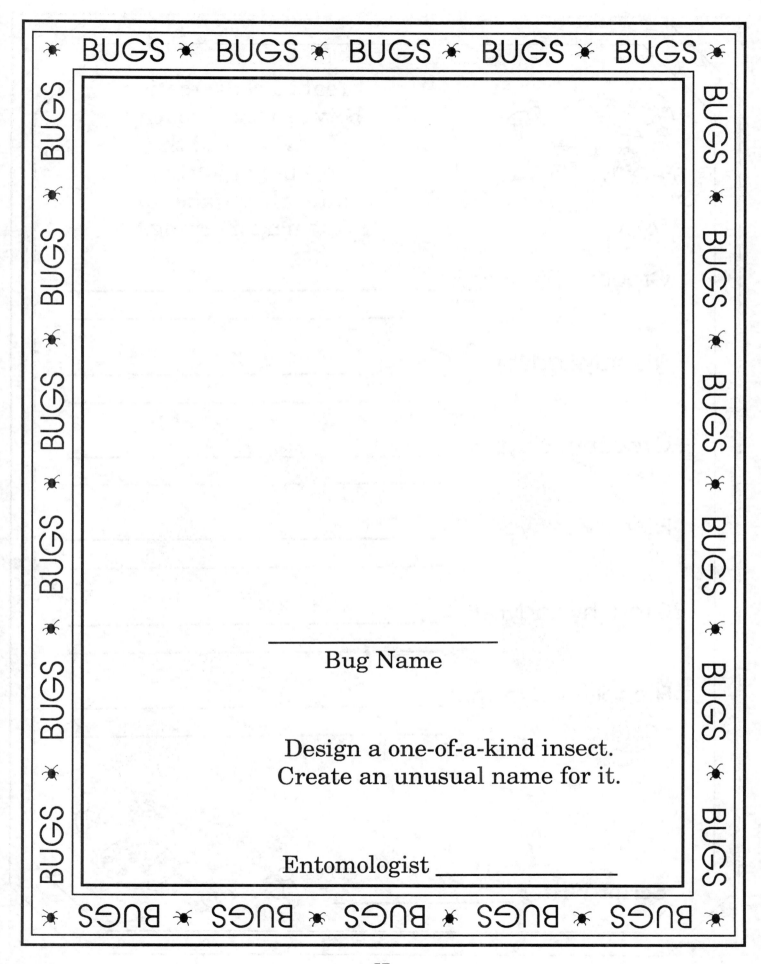

BUGS * BUGS * BUGS * BUGS * BUGS

_____

Bug Name

Design a one-of-a-kind insect.
Create an unusual name for it.

Entomologist _____

GA1393

Create a conversation between the Grouchy Ladybug and the Friendly Ladybug after they wake up the next morning.

Grouchy Ladybug: _____

_____

Friendly Ladybug: _____

_____

Grouchy Ladybug: _____

_____

Friendly Ladybug: _____

_____

Grouchy Ladybug: _____

_____

Friendly Ladybug: _____

_____

Script Writer _____

GA1392

BUGS, BUGS, BUGS RESEARCH

Research Project

✦ Students will discover five to ten facts about a bug.
✦ Students will create a large poster about an insect.

Research Center

✦ The Bugs, Bugs, Bugs Research Center should include:

• a special place in your classroom decorated with an insect theme using items such as a butterfly net, a bug box or jars for displaying live samples.
• insect research resources.
• a laminated copy of the student activity packet (for teacher use and display at the center).

✦ Provide each student with materials for creating a bug poster. Encourage students to draw or make a two-dimensional, cut-paper replica of their bug. Be sure to include the environmental background.

✦ The completed research projects will be large insect posters.

✦ Award each student an Expert Certificate upon completion of the center.

Research Resources

✦ Danks, Hugh. *The Bug Book*. New York: Workman Publishing, 1987.

✦ Day, Jennifer W. *What Is an Insect?* New York: A Golden Book, 1975.

✦ Goor, Ronald, and Millicent E. Selsam. *Backyard Insects*. New York: Scholastic Books, 1981.

✦ Katz, Bobbi. *The Creepy, Crawly Book*. New York: Random House, 1989.

✦ Parker, Nancy, and Joan Wright. *Bugs*. Greenwillow Books, 1987.

GA1393

BUGS, BUGS, BUGS RESEARCH

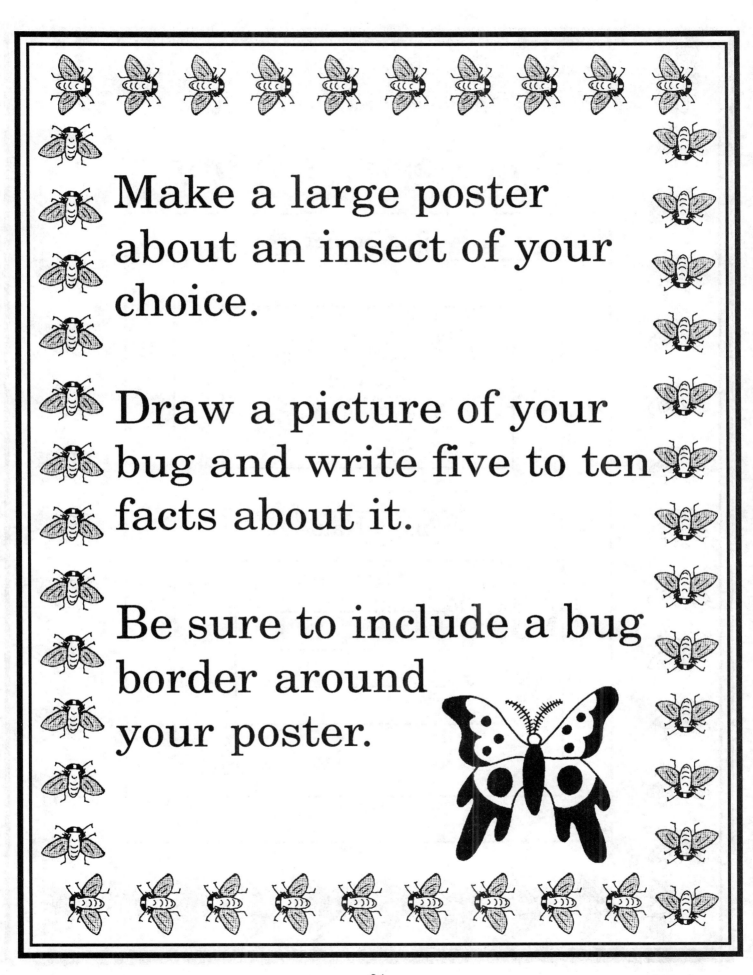

Make a large poster about an insect of your choice.

Draw a picture of your bug and write five to ten facts about it.

Be sure to include a bug border around your poster.

61

GA1393

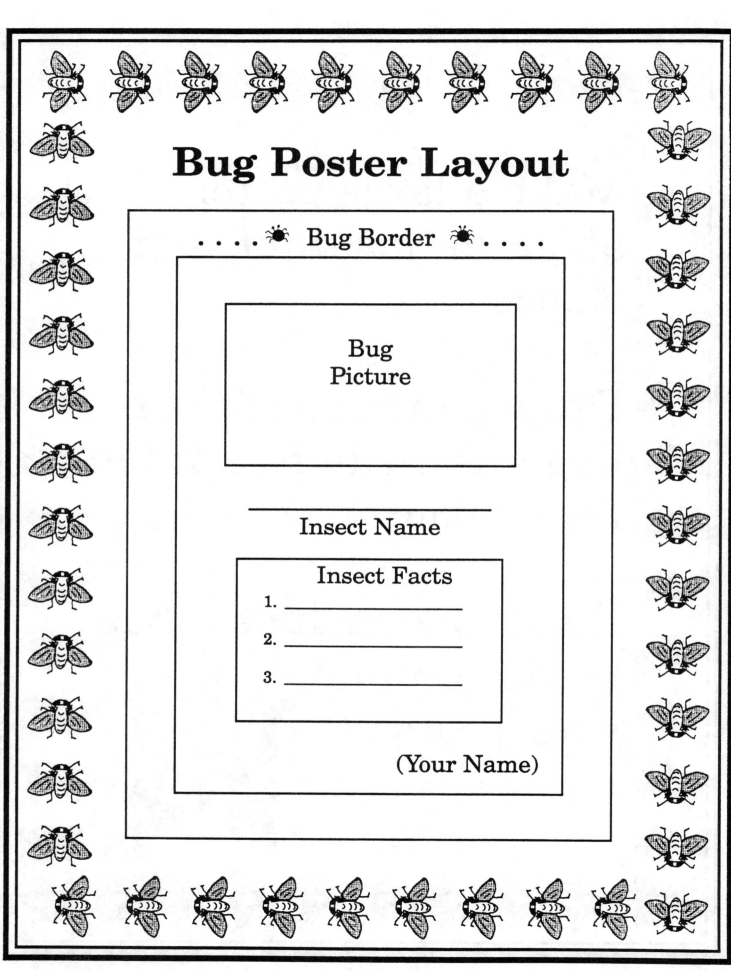

Bug Poster Layout

.....🕷 Bug Border 🕷.....

Bug
Picture

_____
Insect Name

Insect Facts
1. _____
2. _____
3. _____

(Your Name)

62

GA1393

Going Buggy

Take a walk around your backyard, playground, house, school or garden. Draw a picture of two bugs you find on your walk. Look in insect books to find the identity of your buggy friends.

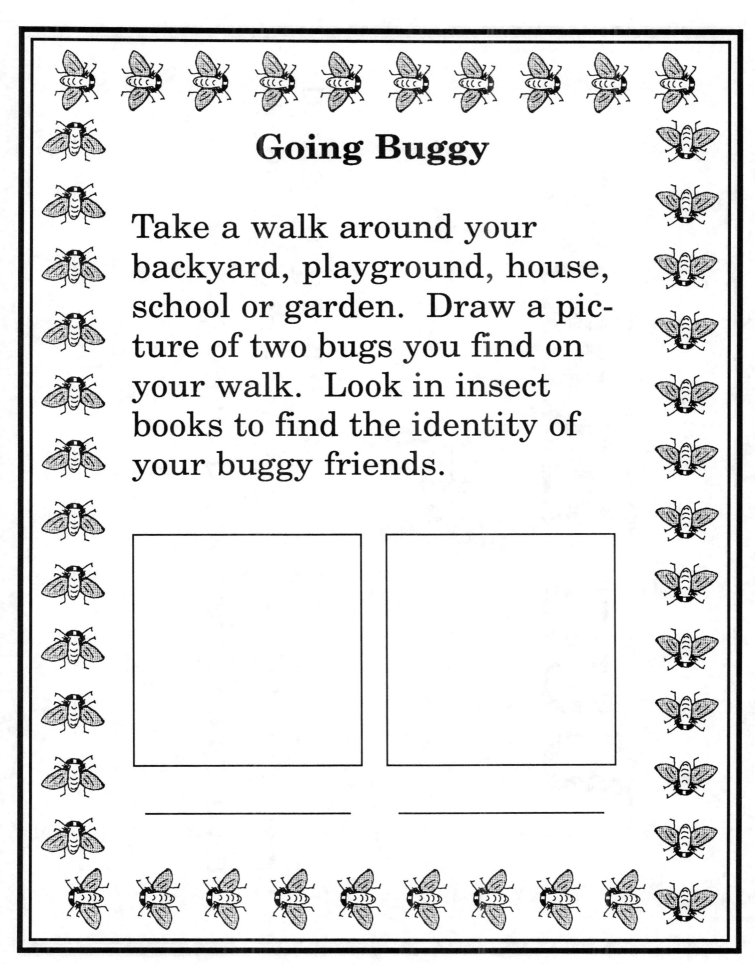

_____   _____

BUG EXPERT

_____ has explored and
investigated the topic of Bugs. Congratulations
on your newly learned knowledge!

Teacher _____

Date _____

HORTON HATCHES THE EGG

Dr. Seuss
Random House, Inc., NY, 1940

Horton the Elephant helps Mayzie, a lazy bird, hatch her egg.

BLOOM'S QUESTIONS

KNOWLEDGE
List three things Mayzie did at the beginning of the story.

COMPREHENSION
Tell how Horton felt at the beginning, middle and end of the story.

APPLICATION
Select a situation from the story and tell how you would have handled it differently.

ANALYSIS
Analyze the story and choose the parts that were funniest, saddest, happiest, etc.

*SYNTHESIS
Design a congratulations card to welcome the Elephant-Bird to the world.

EVALUATION
Judge whether Horton or Mayzie should keep the Elephant-Bird. Share your reason.

CREATIVE THINKING ACTIVITIES

FLUENCY
Brainstorm a long list of birds.

FLEXIBILITY
Divide your list into as many categories as you can. For example: Birds in My Community, Birds that Fly South in Winter, Large Birds, Small Birds, Birds that Cannot Fly. You may need a bird book to help find correct answers.

ORIGINALITY
Choose a bird from your list and select one of its unique features. Combine that feature with your favorite animal. Draw a picture of your new creation. Be sure to give it a name.

*ELABORATION
Elaborate on Mayzie's trip to Palm Beach. List Mayzie's activities for one week.

GA1393

HORTON HATCHES THE EGG

Design a congratulations card to welcome the Elephant-Bird to the world.

Fold a piece of paper in half like a card and glue it here.

Greeting Card Company _____

Elaborate on Mayzie's trip to Palm Beach. List Mayzie's activities for a one-week stay.

Monday: _____

_____

_____

Tuesday: _____

_____

_____

Wednesday: _____

_____

_____

Thursday: _____

_____

_____

Friday: _____

_____

_____

Saturday: _____

_____

_____

Sunday: _____

_____

_____

Vacation Director _____

ELEPHANT EXPLORATIONS RESEARCH

Research Project

✦ Students will research at least six elephant facts.
✦ Students will create an elephant mural.

Research Center

✦ The Elephant Explorations Research Center should include:

- a special place in your classroom decorated with a jungle or circus theme.
- elephant research resources.
- a laminated copy of the student activity packet (for teacher use and display at the center).

✦ Provide each student with a set of elephant shapes including the cover and student directions.

✦ The completed research projects can be displayed as class or individual murals or as shape books.

✦ Award each student an Expert Certificate upon completion of the center.

Research Resources

✦ *Elephants.* Wonder Books: Alan Publishers, Inc., 1981.

✦ "Elephants," *Zoobooks* Magazine. San Diego: Wildlife Education, Ltd., 1986.

✦ McGovern, Ann. *Elephant Baby.* New York: Scholastic Books, Inc., 1982.

✦ Pfeffer, Pierre. *Elephants: Big, Strong, and Wise.* New York: Young Discovery Library, 1987.

✦ Schlein, Miriam. *Elephants.* New York: Aladdin Books, 1990.

GA1393

ELEPHANT EXPLORATIONS RESEARCH

70

GA1393

Answer each elephant question by using books from the library.

Then create a jungle or circus mural using the elephants.

Color and decorate each elephant.

Add details to the background to complete the scene.

Arrange and glue the elephants onto a long piece of paper in a variety of ways: marching in a line trunk to tail, in circus rings, in herds, around a water hole, carrying logs or people.

GA1393

Name the two kinds of elephants.

GA1393

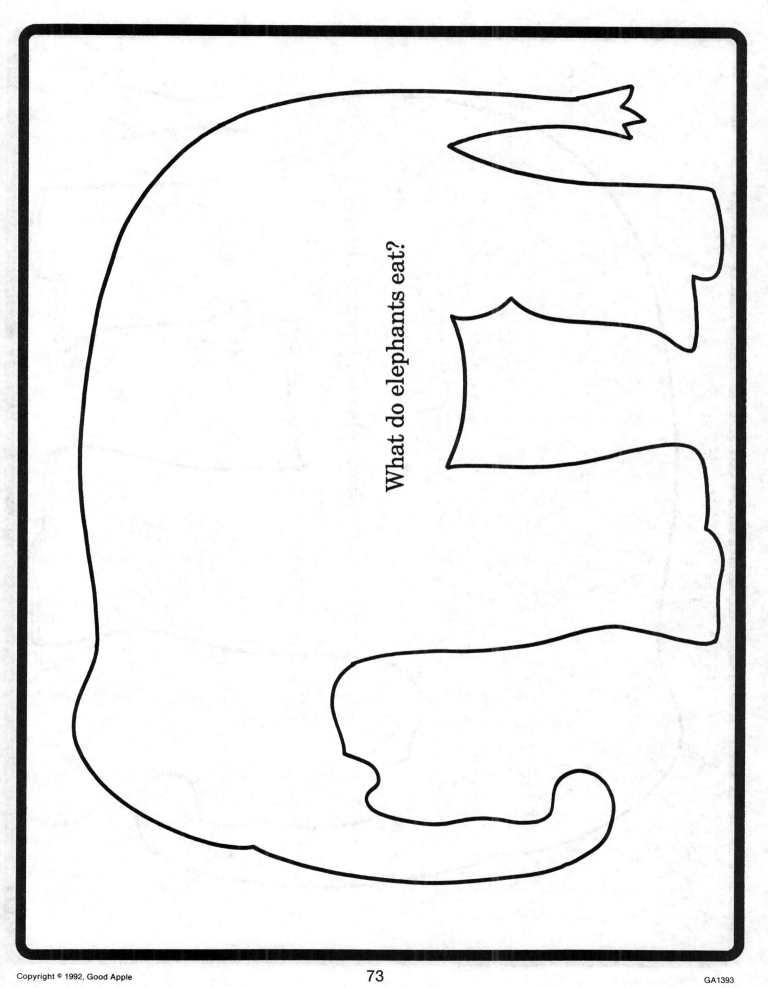

What do elephants eat?

GA1393

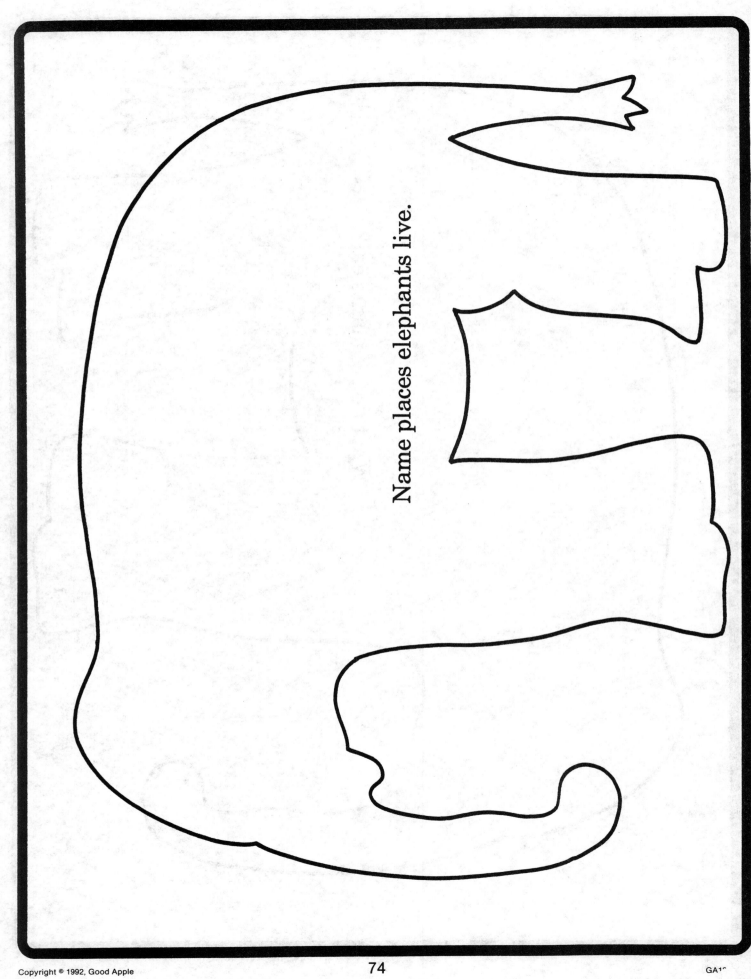

Name places elephants live.

74

The elephant's trunk has many uses.
Name as many as you can find.

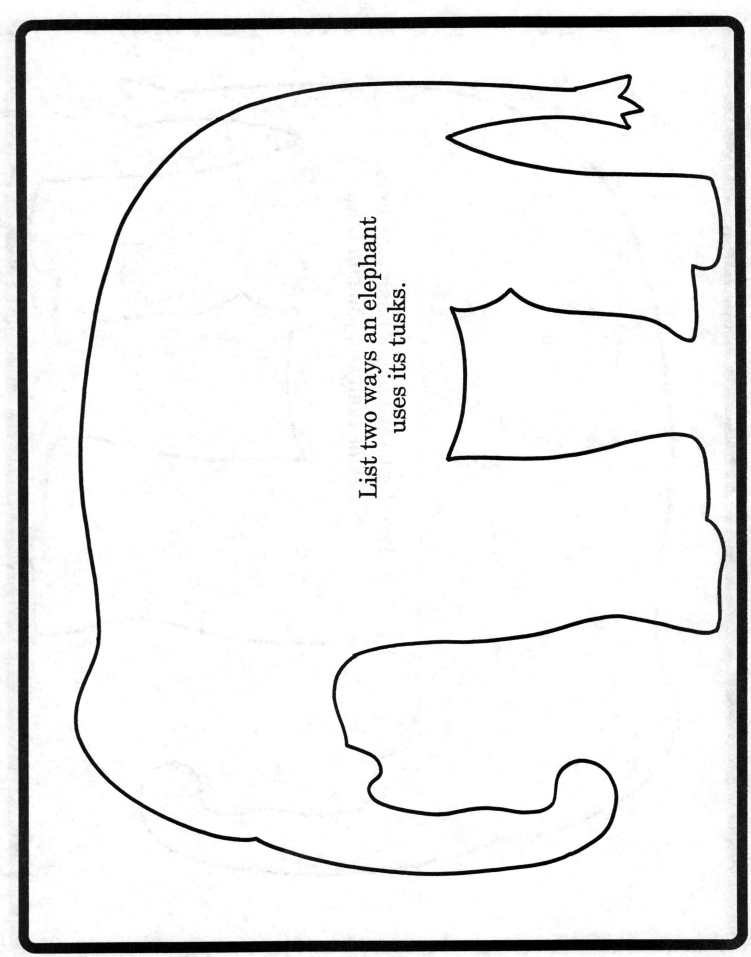

List two ways an elephant uses its tusks.

76

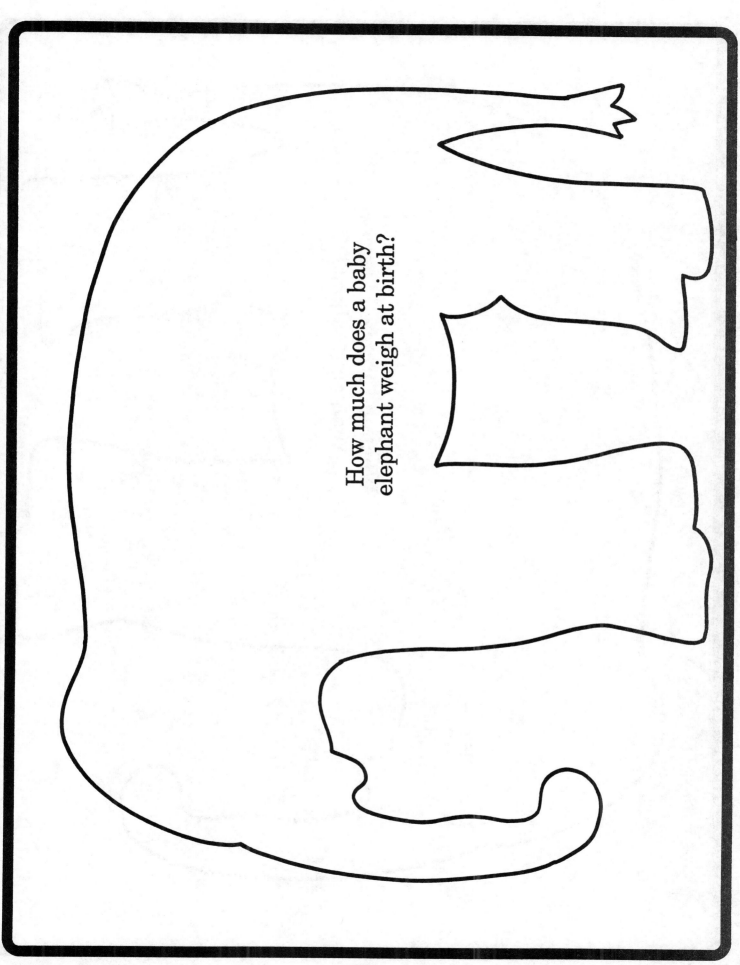

How much does a baby elephant weigh at birth?

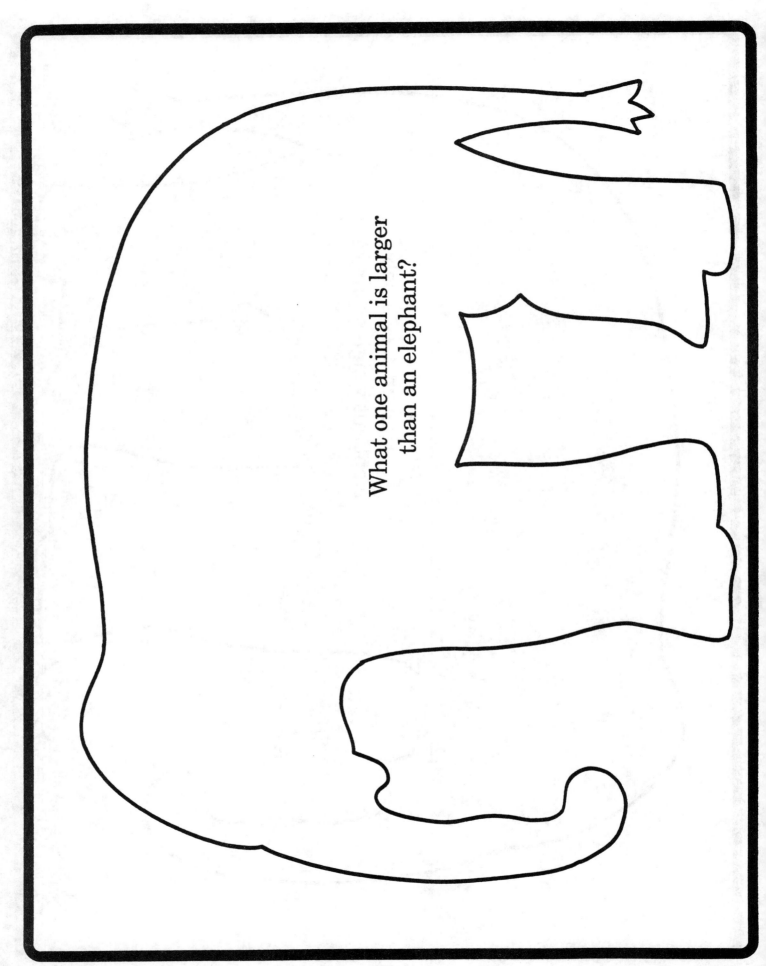

What one animal is larger than an elephant?

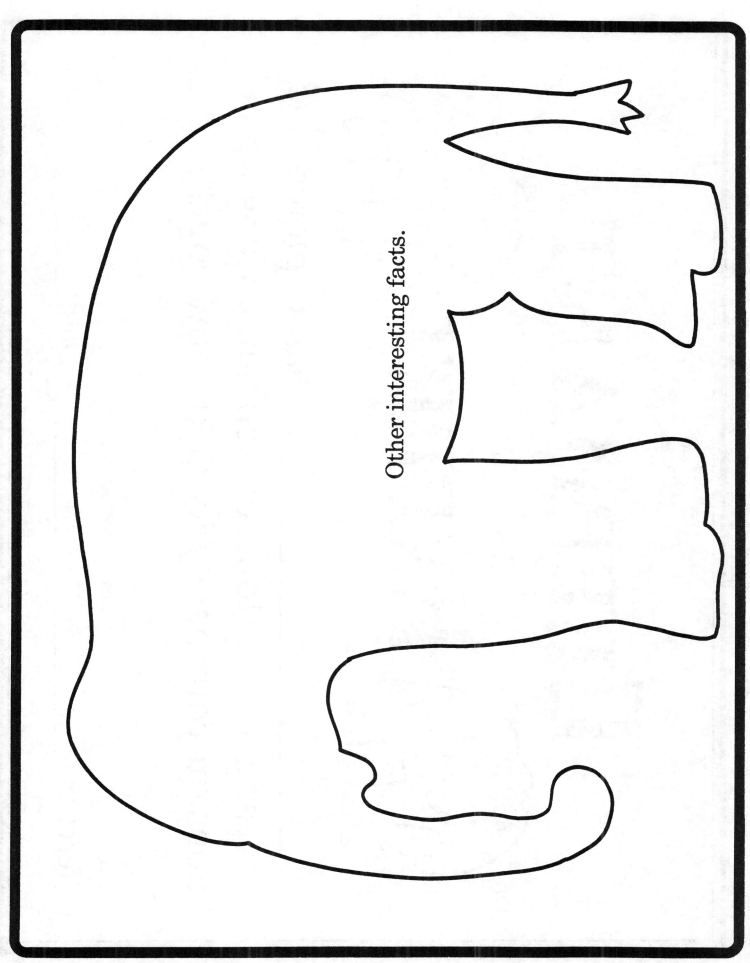

Other interesting facts.

79

GA1393

ELEPHANT EXPERT

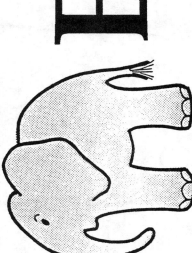

_____ has explored and investigated the topic of Elephants. Congratulations on your newly learned knowledge!

Teacher _____

Date _____

80

A HOUSE FOR HERMIT CRAB

Eric Carle
Picture Book Studios, NY, 1987

Hermit Crab has a problem: he keeps outgrowing things.
This book explores his adventures.

BLOOM'S QUESTIONS

KNOWLEDGE
Describe Hermit Crab's house at the beginning of the story.

COMPREHENSION
Explain why Hermit Crab wanted to decorate his house.

APPLICATION
If you were Hermit Crab, how would you decorate the house?

ANALYSIS
Compare Hermit Crab's house to your house.

*SYNTHESIS
Create a new house for Hermit Crab. Decorate it with items *not* found in the sea.
Draw a picture of it.

EVALUATION
Decide how you feel about Hermit Crab's decision to give his house to the little crab.

CREATIVE THINKING ACTIVITIES

FLUENCY
Brainstorm a long list of things found in the sea.

*FLEXIBILITY
Hermit Crab used a shell for his house. What else can a shell be used for?

ORIGINALITY
Create an underwater mural using your list of things found under the sea.

ELABORATION
Elaborate on the end of the story by drawing a picture of Hermit Crab's new house.

GA1393

A HOUSE FOR HERMIT CRAB

Create a new house for Hermit Crab. Decorate
it with items *not* found in the sea.

Crab House Architect _____

83

Illustrate a unique and unusual use for a starfish shell.

Shell Innovator _____

HERMIT CRAB OBSERVATIONAL RESEARCH

Research Project

- ✦ Students will observe live hermit crabs.
- ✦ Students will record and answer questions about their observations.

Research Center

- ✦ The Hermit Crab Observational Research Center should include:

  - a special place in your classroom with an ocean motif.
  - hermit crab research resources.
  - a laminated copy of the student activity packet (for teacher use and display at the center).
  - a hermit crab in an aquarium (hermit crabs are very inexpensive and can be found at most pet stores).
  - a magnifying glass.

- ✦ Provide each student with the hermit crab activity packet including the cover and student directions.

- ✦ The completed research projects can be displayed on a bulletin board near the center, in the library for others to read or taken to a local pet store.

- ✦ Award each student an Expert Certificate upon completion of the center.

Research Resources

- ✦ Holling, Clancy. *Pagoo*. New York: Houghton Mifflin, 1957.

- ✦ Johnson, Sylvia. *Hermit Crabs*. Minneapolis: Lerner Publications Co., 1989.

- ✦ Nash, Paul J. *Land Hermit Crabs*. New Jersey: Tropical Fish Hobbyist, 1976.

HERMIT CRAB OBSERVA- TIONAL RESEARCH

GA1393

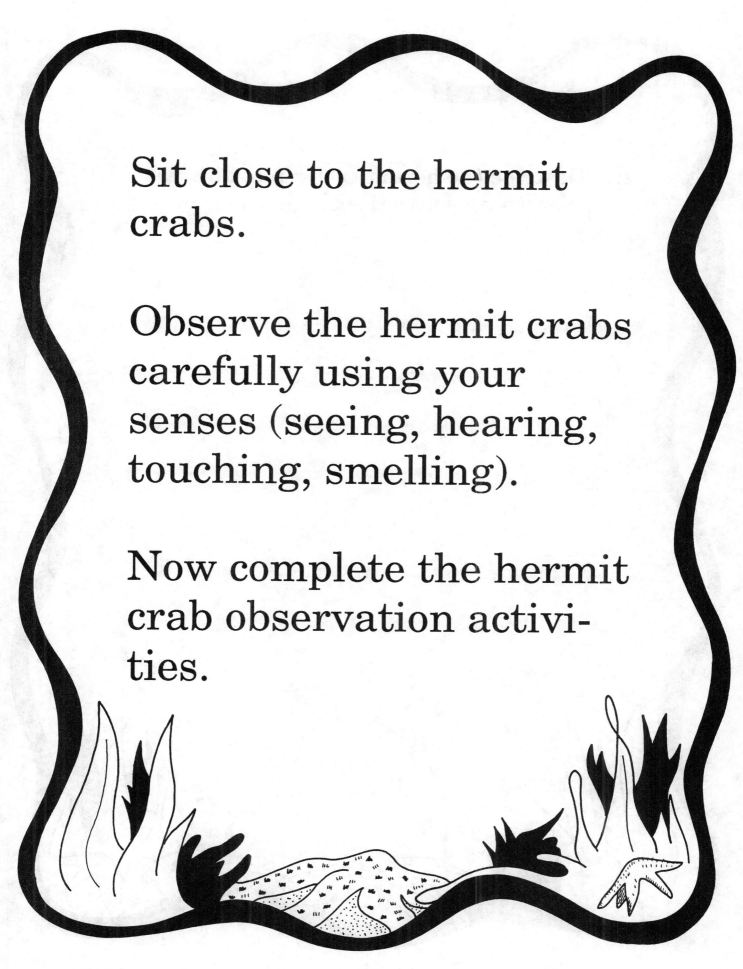

Sit close to the hermit crabs.

Observe the hermit crabs carefully using your senses (seeing, hearing, touching, smelling).

Now complete the hermit crab observation activities.

GA1393

1. Describe the hermit crabs in detail. List everything you notice about them.

2. How are they alike?

3. How are they different?

4. What do you think is most interesting about them?

GA1393

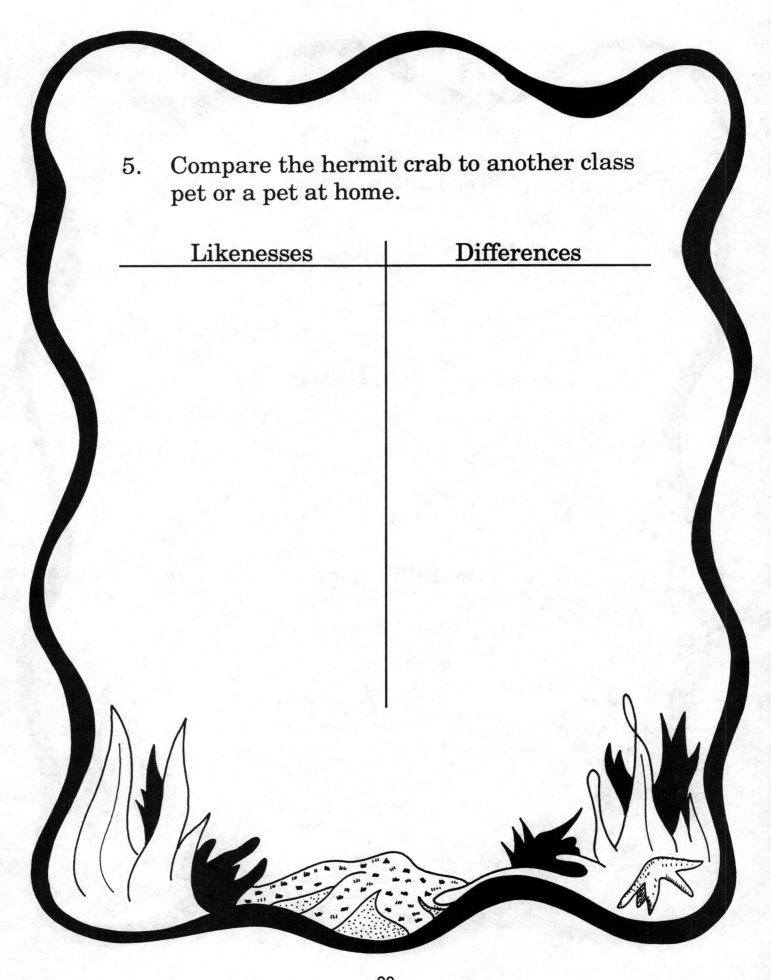

5. Compare the hermit crab to another class pet or a pet at home.

Likenesses	Differences

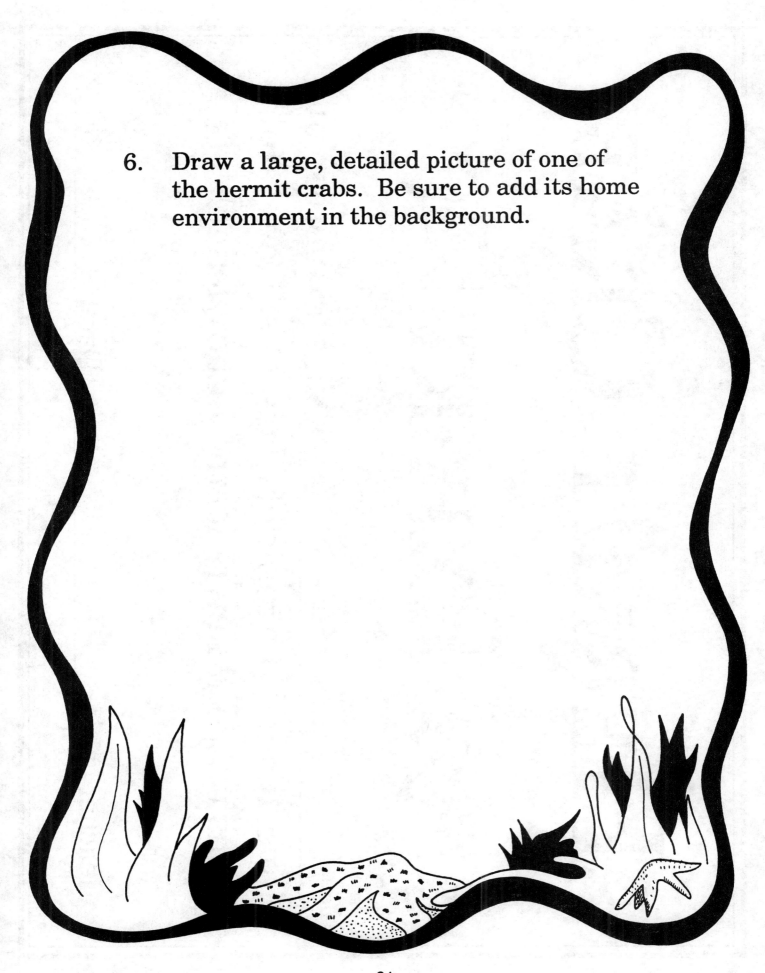

6. Draw a large, detailed picture of one of the hermit crabs. Be sure to add its home environment in the background.

GA1393

HERMIT CRAB EXPERT

_____ has explored and investigated the topic of Class Pets. Congratulations on your newly learned knowledge!

Teacher _____

Date _____

KATY AND THE BIG SNOW

Virginia Lee Burton
Scholastic, Inc., NY, 1943

Katy, the tractor, is very big and can do many things. As a snowplow, she helps keep the city working when a blizzard hits.

BLOOM'S QUESTIONS

KNOWLEDGE
What type of vehicle was Katy?

COMPREHENSION
Why did the Highway Department need Katy when the blizzard struck the city?

APPLICATION
Share a winter snowstorm adventure from your own life.

ANALYSIS
Compare Katy's work in the winter season to her work in the summer season.

*SYNTHESIS
Suppose the snow was too big for Katy. What would they have done without Katy?

EVALUATION
Do you think it was a good idea for the City of Geoppolis to rely on Katy for the city's snow emergencies? Why or why not?

CREATIVE THINKING ACTIVITIES

FLUENCY
Make a list of all the problems a large snowstorm can create.

FLEXIBILITY
Look at your list of problems created by the snow. Select the most frightening problem and draw a picture of it.

*ORIGINALITY
Invent a new way for snow to be removed from the streets.

*ELABORATION
Many city trucks are painted the same plain color. Elaborate on one of the trucks in the story. Give it an interesting coat of paint and add design details.

GA1393

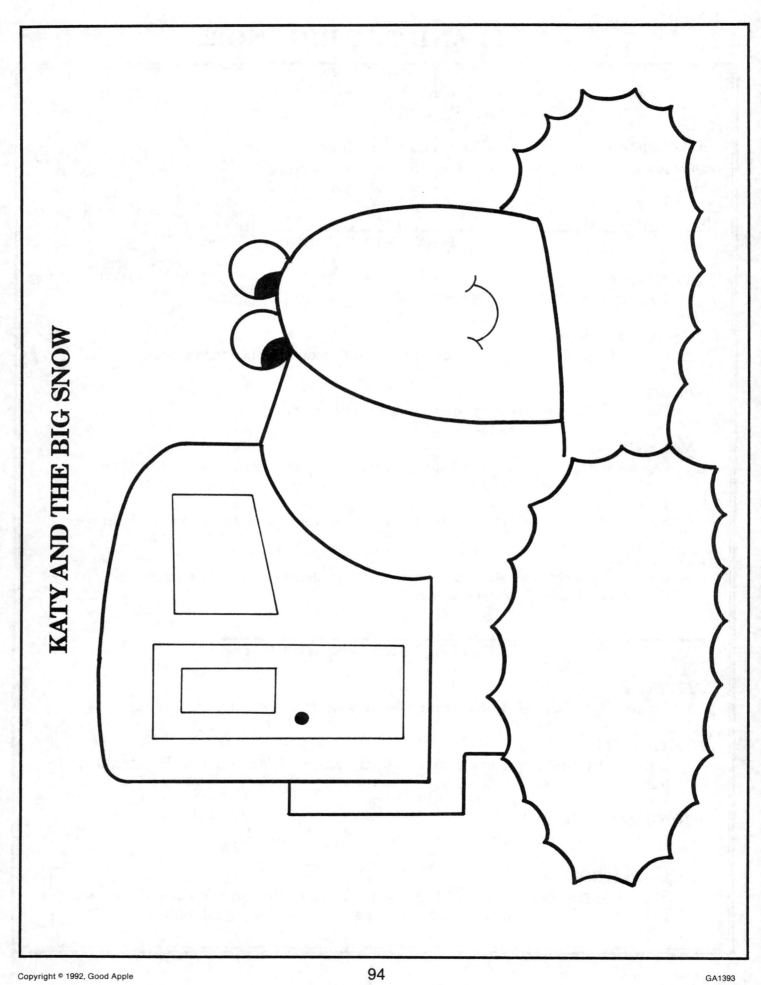

KATY AND THE BIG SNOW

94

GA1393

Invent a new way for snow to be
removed from the streets.

Snow Remover _____

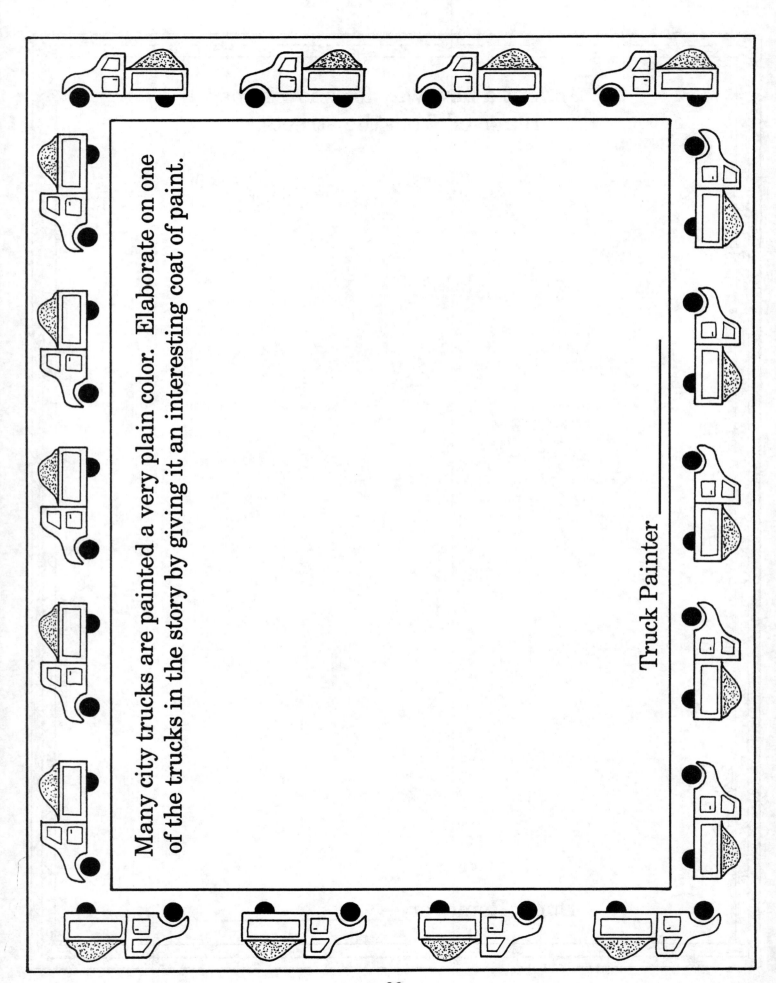

Many city trucks are painted a very plain color. Elaborate on one of the trucks in the story by giving it an interesting coat of paint.

Truck Painter

96

GA1393

TRUCKIN' ALONG RESEARCH

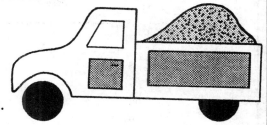

Research Project

◆ Students will research eight kinds of trucks.
◆ Students will create a truck shape encyclopedia.

Research Center

◆ The Truckin' Along Research Center should include:

  • a special place in your classroom decorated with a truck theme, including toy trucks, fiction truck books, hard hat, truck puzzles, thermos and lunch box.
  • truck/vehicle research resources.
  • a laminated copy of the student activity packet (for teacher use and display at the center).

◆ Provide each student with a copy of the truck research shapes including the cover and student directions.

◆ The completed research project can be displayed as individual truck encyclopedias or as a highway mural.

◆ Award each student an Expert Certificate upon completion of the center.

Research Resources

◆ Bushey, Jerry. *Monster Trucks and Other Giant Machines on Wheels.* New York: Carolrhoda, 1985.

◆ Crews, Donald. *Truck.* New York: Puffin, 1985.

◆ Gibbons, Gail. *Trucks.* New York: Thomas Y. Crowell, 1981.

◆ Potter, Tony. *See How It Works: Trucks.* New York: Aladdin Books, 1989.

◆ Robbins, Ken. *Trucks of Every Sort.* New York: Crown, 1981.

TRUCKIN'
ALONG
RESEARCH

Write and draw a definition for each piece of heavy equipment owned and operated by most cities. Assemble into a truck encyclopedia or highway mural.

Contact your local Department of Public Works to discover which trucks are used and owned by your city.

GA1393

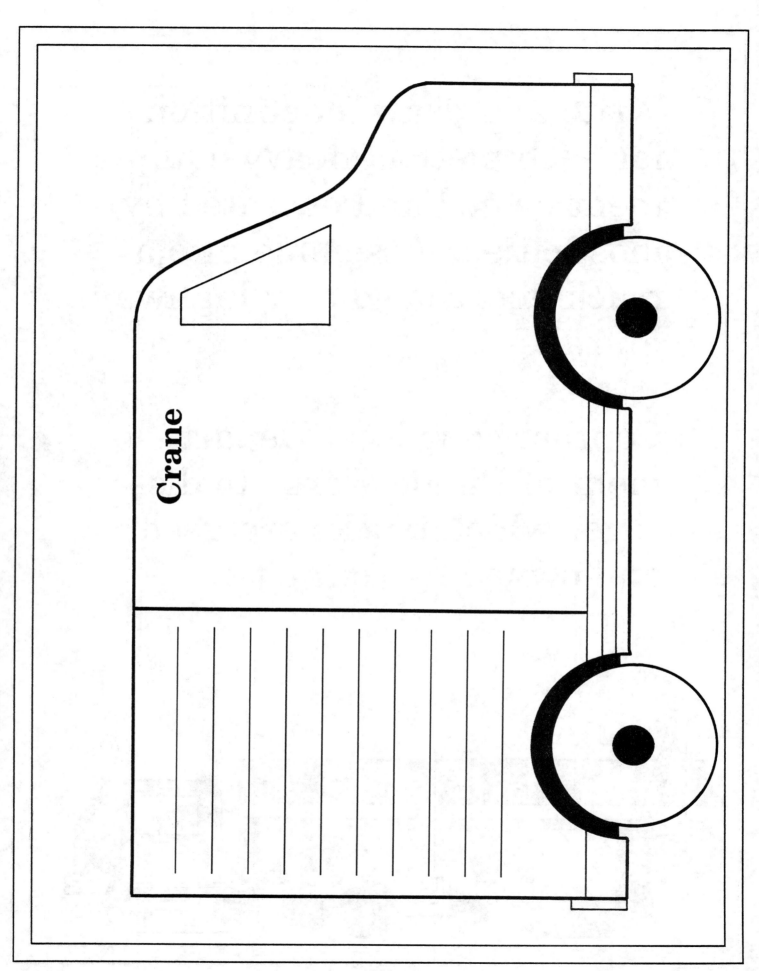

Crane

100

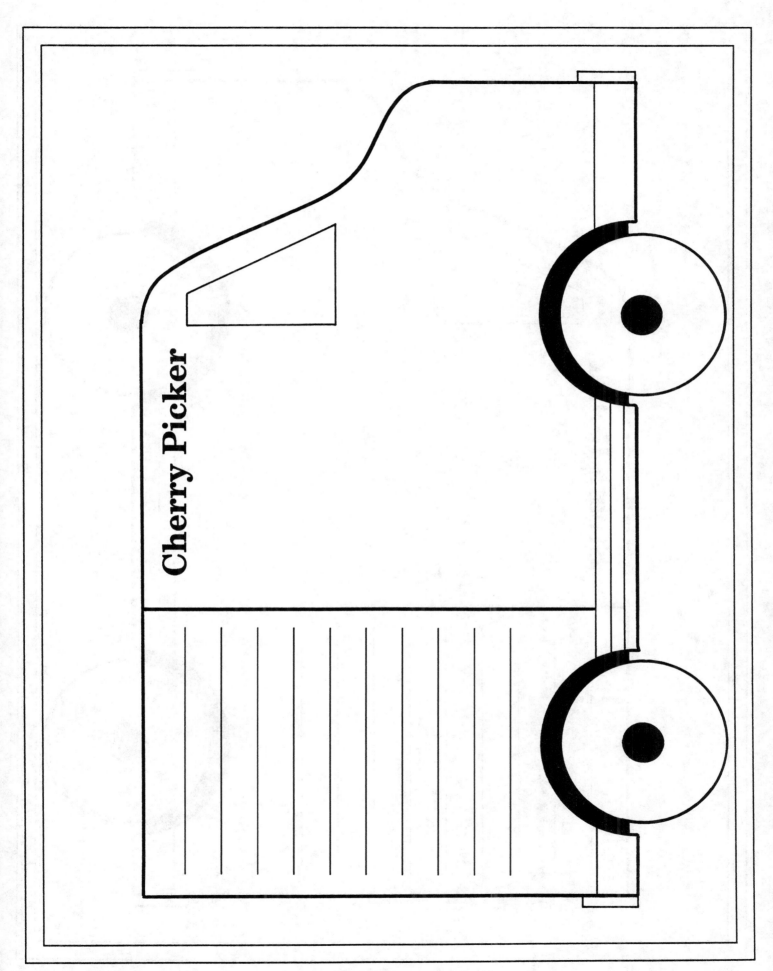

Cherry Picker

101

GA1393

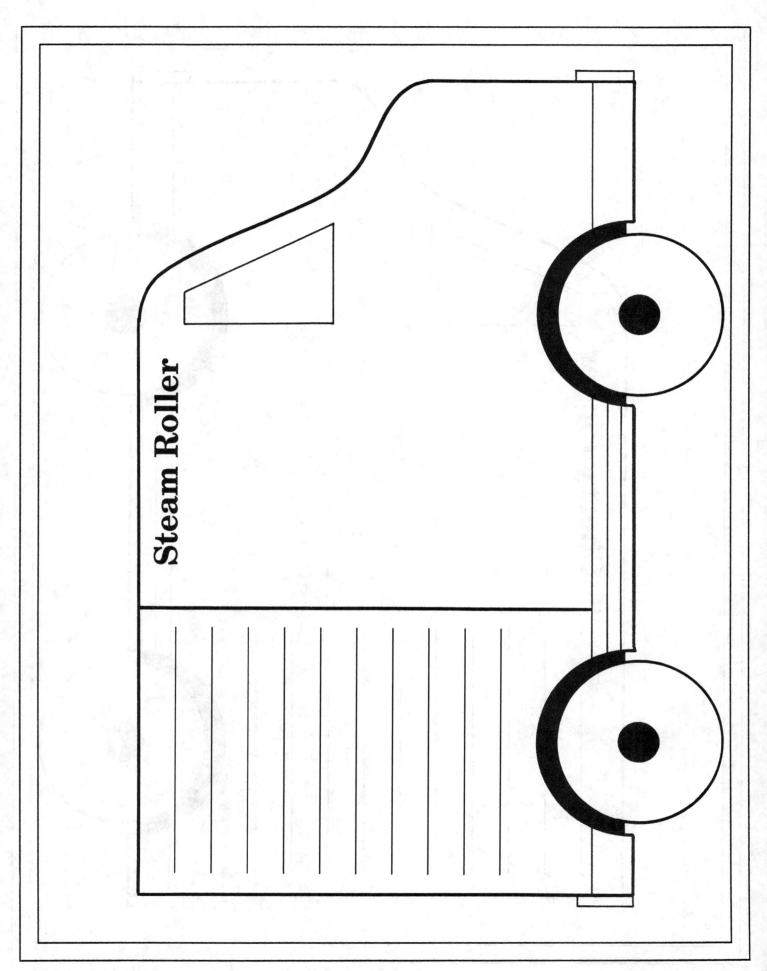

Steam Roller

GA1393

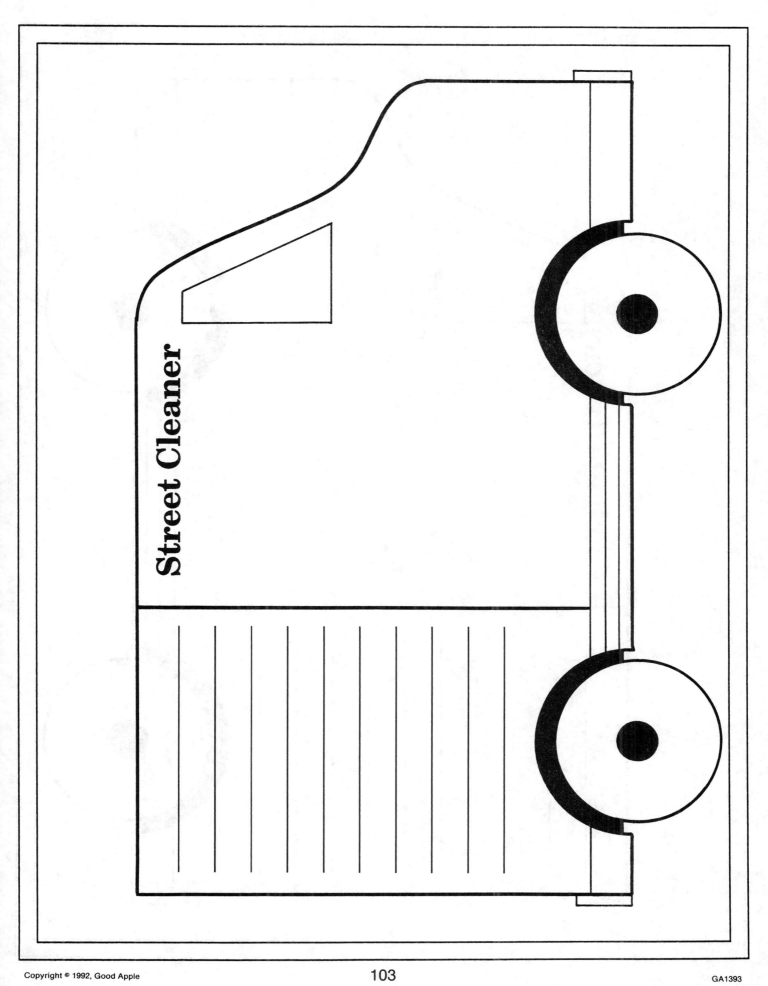

Street Cleaner

103

GA1393

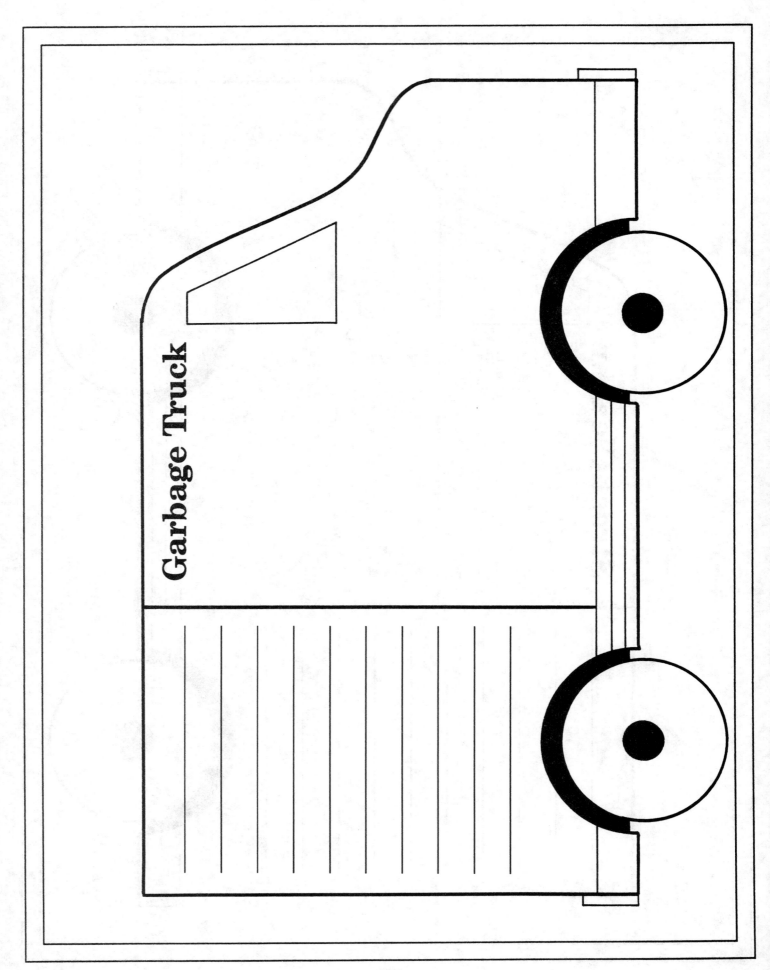

Garbage Truck

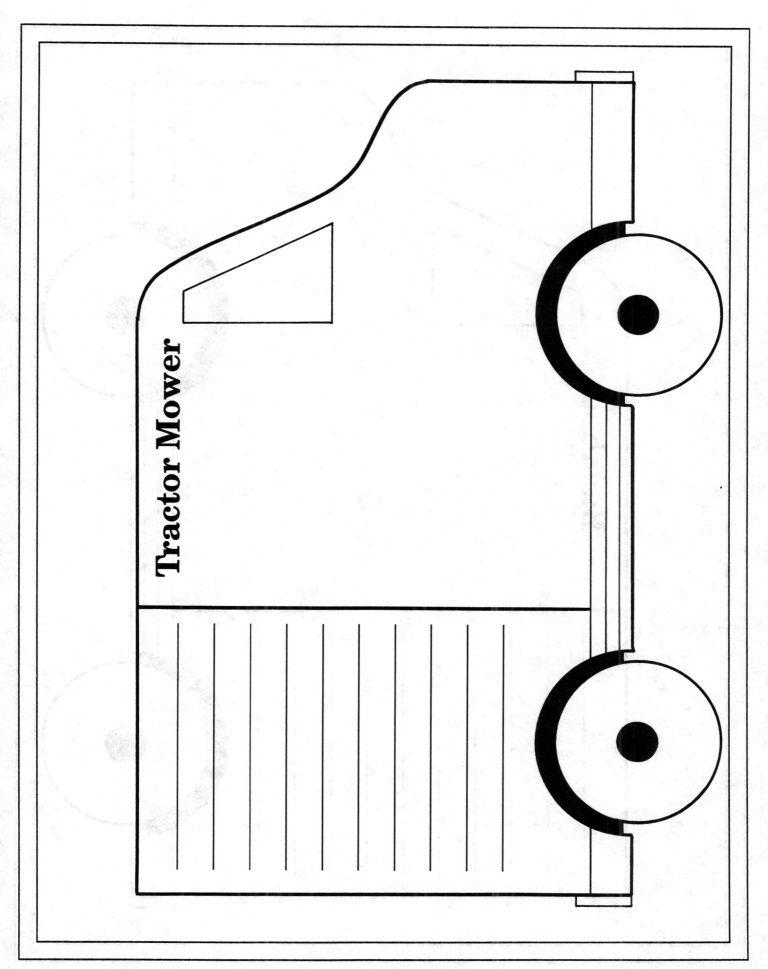

Tractor Mower

105

GA1393

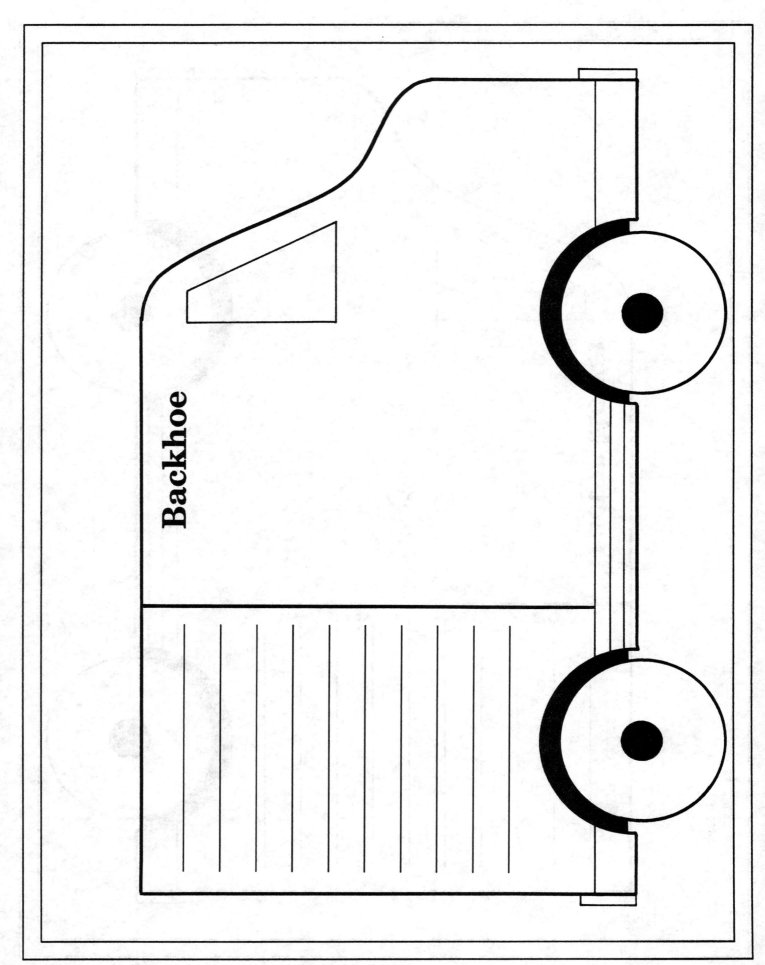

Backhoe

GA1393

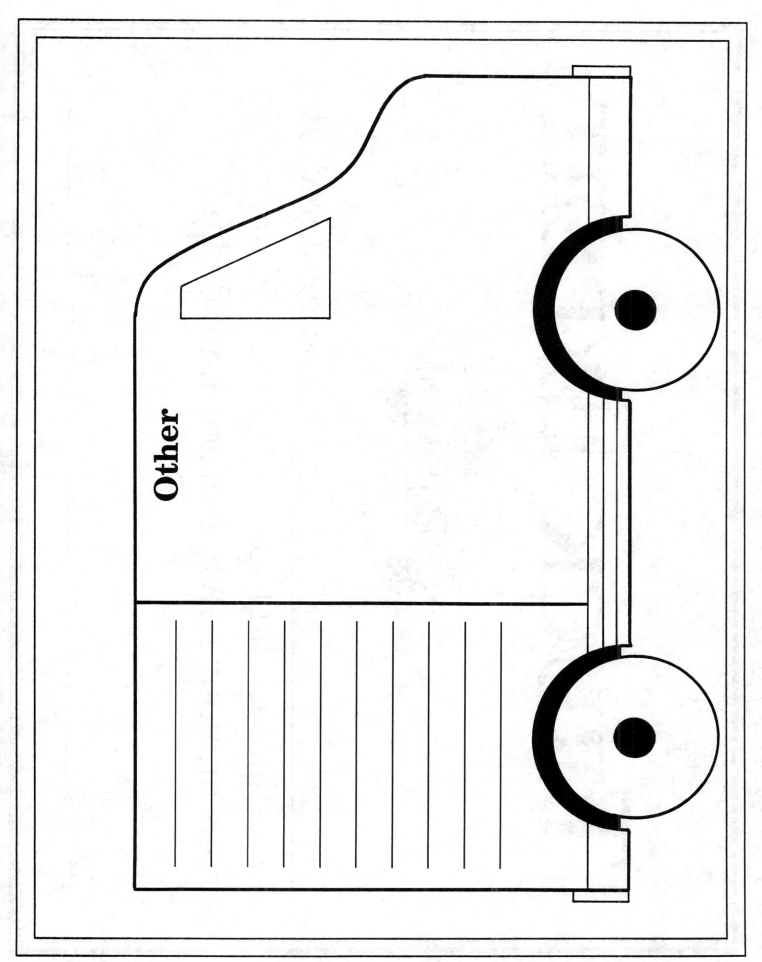

Other

GA1393

TRUCK EXPERT

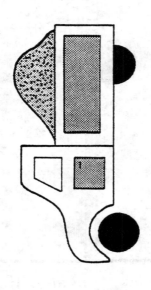

_____ has explored and investigated the topic of Vehicles. Congratulations on your newly learned knowledge!

Teacher _____

Date _____

MADELINE

Ludwig Bemelmans
Scholastic, Inc., NY, 1939

Madeline, a young girl in Paris, awakens in the middle of the night and a trip to the hospital follows.

BLOOM'S QUESTIONS

KNOWLEDGE
What is the setting of the story?

COMPREHENSION
Name three things Madeline enjoyed doing in the story.

APPLICATION
Share an experience from your own life in which you were frightened.

ANALYSIS
Compare Madeline's living arrangements with your own.

SYNTHESIS
Think of a new reason the girls might have been crying at the end of the story.

EVALUATION
Decide whether you think Madeline's life is a good or bad life to lead.

CREATIVE THINKING ACTIVITIES

FLUENCY
Twelve little girls lived in the old house in Paris. Name as many things as you can that come in a dozen.

FLEXIBILITY
Draw a picture of another way the twelve little girls could have slept in the bedroom, eaten at the table or walked together, other than in two lines.

*ORIGINALITY
Design a new uniform for the girls to wear at a new occasion.

*ELABORATION
Tell about the next field trip adventure you think the girls will have.

GA1393

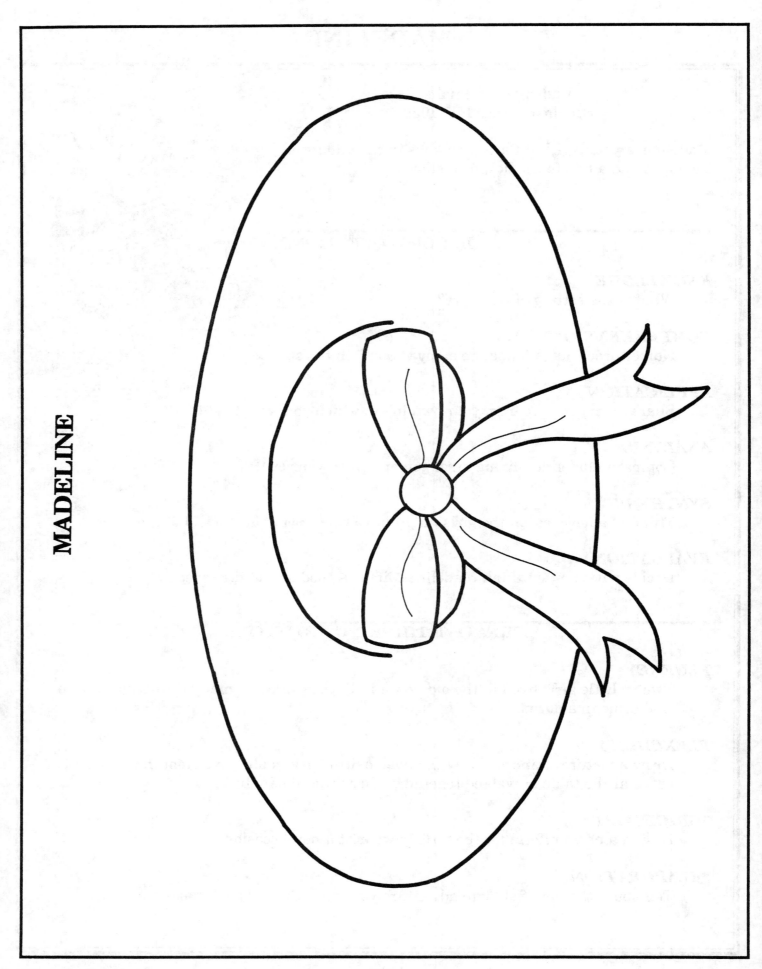

MADELINE

110

Design a new uniform for the girls for a new occasion. Dress the Madeline paper doll in your new creation.

Tailor _____

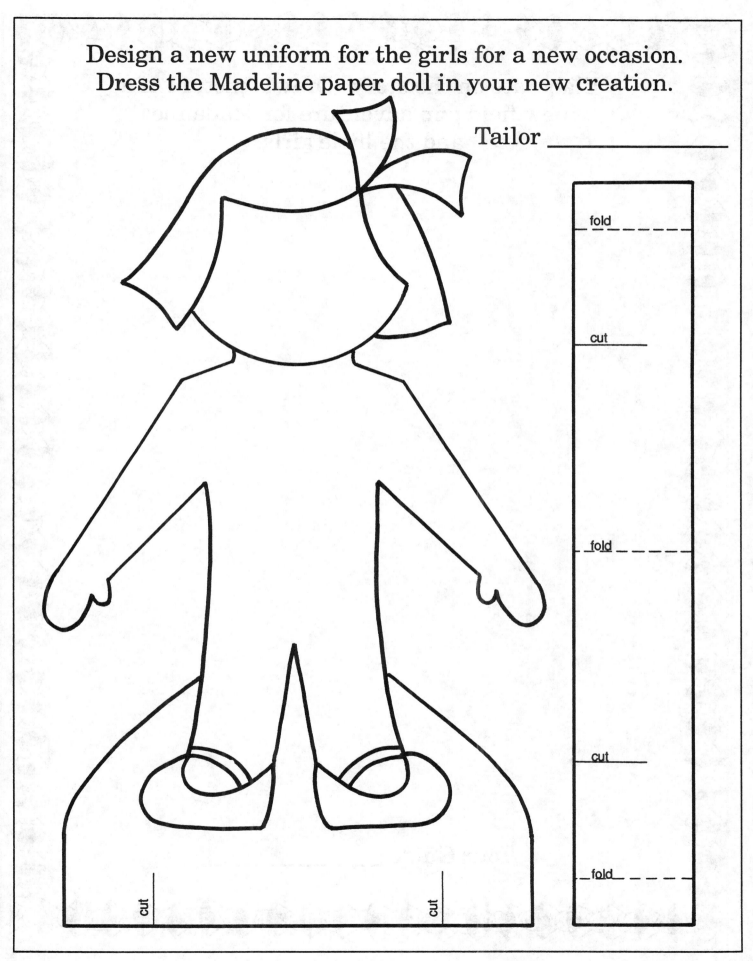

fold

cut

fold

cut

fold

cut

cut

111

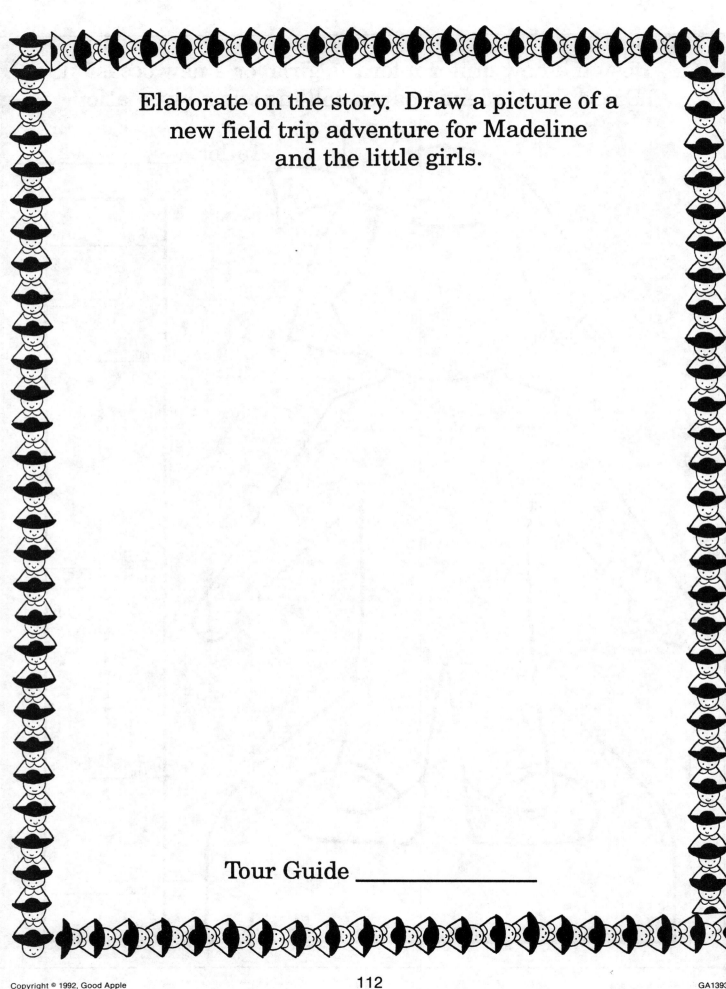

Elaborate on the story. Draw a picture of a
new field trip adventure for Madeline
and the little girls.

Tour Guide _____

PRIMARILY PARIS RESEARCH

Research Project

✦ Students will research twelve facts on Paris.
✦ Students will create a Paris photo album.

Research Center

✦ The Primarily Paris Research Center should include:

  • a special place in your classroom decorated with a French motif, including travel books about France, French cookbooks, French travel posters and a French dictionary.
  • Paris/France research resources.
  • a laminated copy of the student activity packet (for teacher use and display at the center).

✦ Provide each student with a copy of the Paris photo album research shapes including the cover and student directions.

✦ The completed research projects can be displayed as scrapbooks, travel brochures or travel journals.

✦ Award each student an Expert Certificate upon completion of the center.

Research Resources

✦ Champion, Neil. *Countries of the World Facts.* Tulsa, Oklahoma: EDC Publishing, 1986.

✦ Liftshitz, Danielle. *France, The Land and Its People.* Morristown, N.J.: Silver Burdett Co., 1981.

✦ Moss, Peter, and Thelma Palmer. *Enchantment of the World: France.* Chicago: Children's Press, 1986.

✦ Norbrook, Dominique. *Passport to France.* New York: Franklin Watts, 1986.

GA1393

PRIMARILY PARIS RESEARCH

114

GA1393

Madeline lives in Paris and you have just returned from visiting her.

Use books in the library to help you remember what you and Madeline saw in Paris.

Draw pictures of your photographs for an album on Paris.

Here is a picture of me saying hello in French.

Here is one of my favorite churches that we visited.

This is a picture of the Eiffel Tower.

This is one of the parks we visited.

There were several types of buildings in Paris.
Here are two I especially liked.

GA1393

Here is a popular French food.

This is a painting we saw at the
famous museum, The Louvre.

Here is a famous river that runs through Paris.

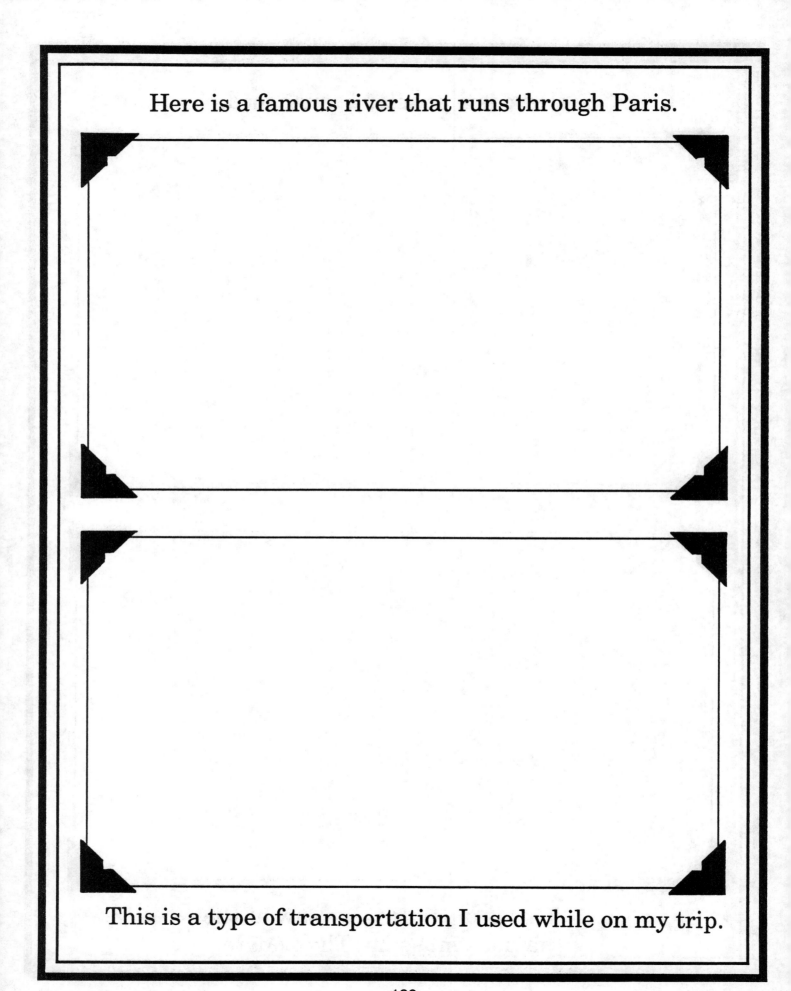

This is a type of transportation I used while on my trip.

GA1393

This is the type of money I used to buy souvenirs.

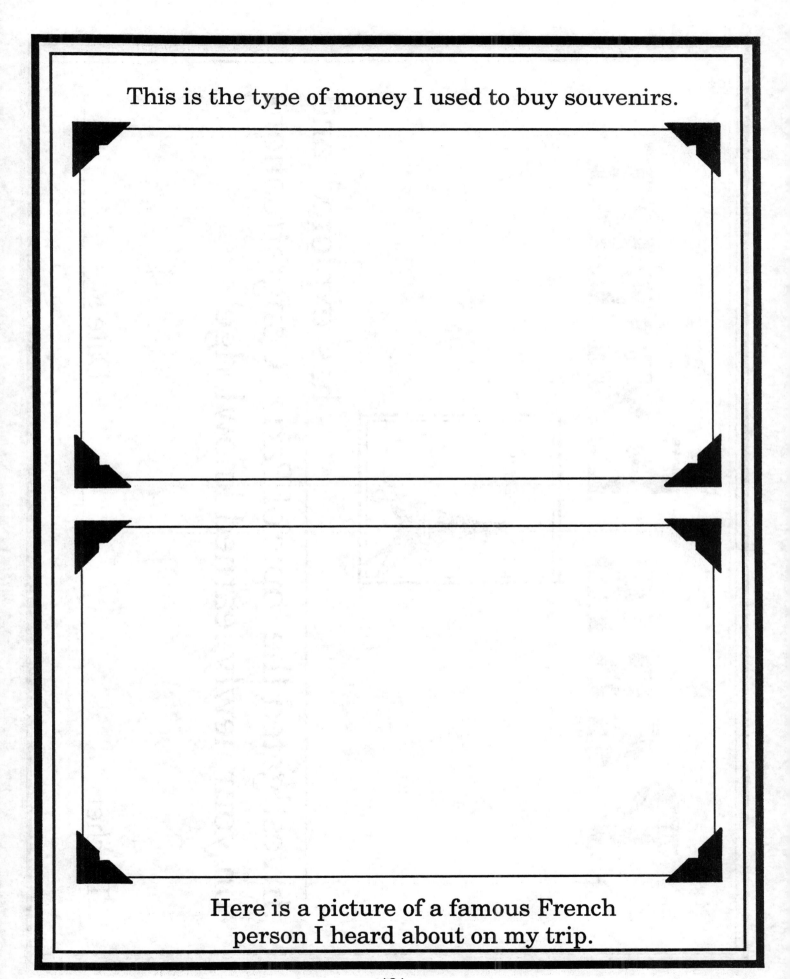

Here is a picture of a famous French
person I heard about on my trip.

PARIS EXPERT

PARIS

_____ has explored and investigated the topic of Paris. Congratulations on your newly learned knowledge!

Teacher _____

Date _____

MISS NELSON HAS A FIELD DAY

Harry Allard and James Marshall
Houghton Mifflin Co., Boston, 1985

Miss Nelson and Miss Viola Swamp come to the rescue of
the Horace B. Smedley School's football team.

BLOOM'S QUESTIONS

KNOWLEDGE
What was the principal's name in the story?

COMPREHENSION
Explain the last page of the story.

APPLICATION
If you were a member of the football team, how would you react to Coach Swamp?

ANALYSIS
Identify how Miss Viola Swamp was an effective coach.

SYNTHESIS
Predict what would have happened if the Horace B. Smedley football team had lost.

EVALUATION
Decide whether Coach Swamp is a good person.

CREATIVE THINKING ACTIVITIES

FLUENCY
List as many sports as you can.

***FLEXIBILITY**
Divide your sports list into categories: Team Sports, Individual Sports, Professional
Sports, Olympic Sports, etc.

***ORIGINALITY**
Design a new football uniform for the Horace B. Smedley School.

ELABORATION
Develop a conversation between Barbara and Miss Nelson at the end of the story.

GA1393

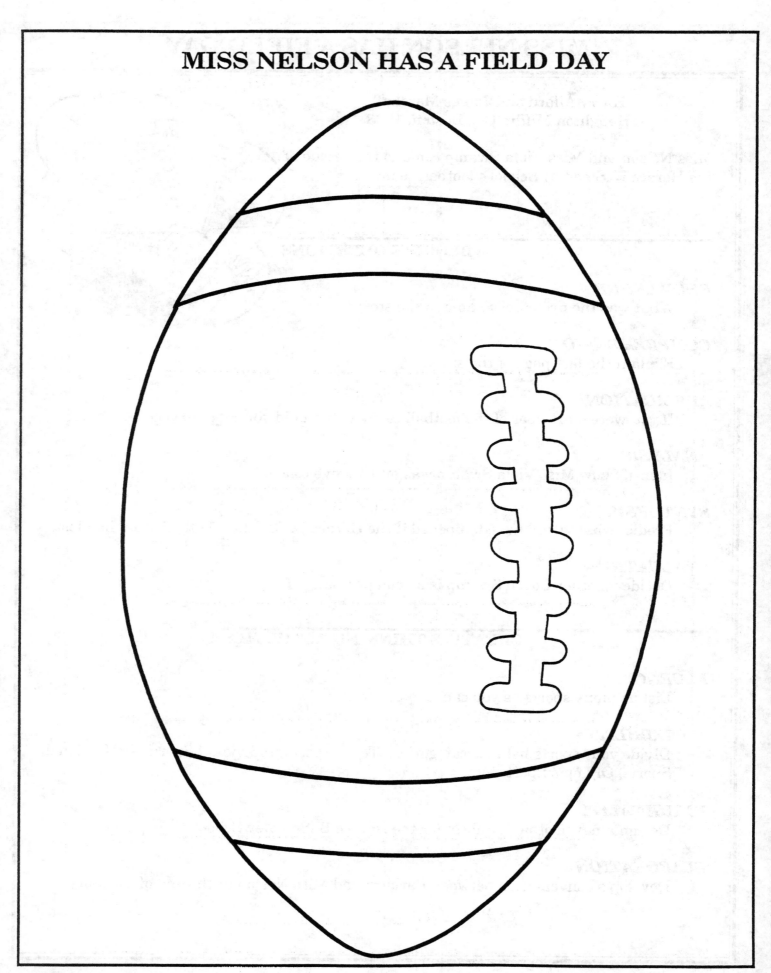

Divide your sports list into categories.

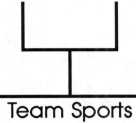

Team Sports

10 —————————————— 10
Individual Sports

20 —————————————— 20
Professional Sports

30 —————————————— 30
Olympic Sports

40 —————————————— 40
Other

50 —————————————— 50

Sports Fan _____

GA1393

Design a new football uniform for
the Horace B. Smedley School.

Uniform Designer _____

126

FOOTBALL FEVER RESEARCH

Research Project

✦ Students will research nine football terms.
✦ Students will create a football dictionary and an informational football collage.

Research Center

✦ The Football Fever Research Center should include:

   • a special place in your classroom decorated with articles from your favorite football team such as hats, T-shirts, pennants, buttons, etc.
   • football research resources.
   • a laminated copy of the student activity packet (for teacher use and display at the center).
   • a dictionary.
   • several sports magazines and/or newspapers that can be cut up.

✦ Provide each student with a set of blank football shapes including the cover and student directions.

✦ The completed research project can be displayed as individual dictionaries on rings to be hung in the gym during Super Bowl Season.

✦ Award each student an Expert Certificate upon completion of the center.

Research Resources

✦ Barrett, Norman. *Football*. London: Franklin Watts, 1988.

✦ Greene, Carol. *I Can Be a Football Player*. Chicago: Children's Press, 1984.

✦ Harris, Richard. *I Can Read About Football*. Mahwah, New Jersey: Troll Associates, 1977.

✦ Any magazine or newspaper article related to football.

GA1393

FOOTBALL
FEVER
RESEARCH

128

Create a Football Dictionary using the words on the next page.

Use football books to find your definitions.

Use the football shape for your pages.

Decorate a cover and assemble your pages into a football dictionary.

Define each word and use it in a sentence with your classmates' names.

hike   interception   tackle

scrimmage   fumble   coach

penalty   Super Bowl   punt

quarterback   field goal

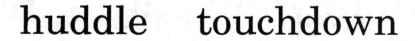

huddle   touchdown

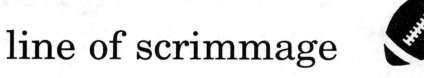

line of scrimmage

EXTRA POINTS!!!

Complete an Extra Points page by cutting out newspaper and magazine words and pictures related to football.

Glue the words and pictures onto a football shape. Overlap them to cover all the spaces.

Give your collage a title.

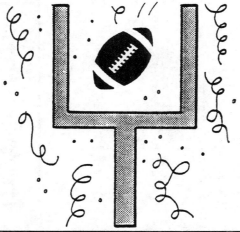

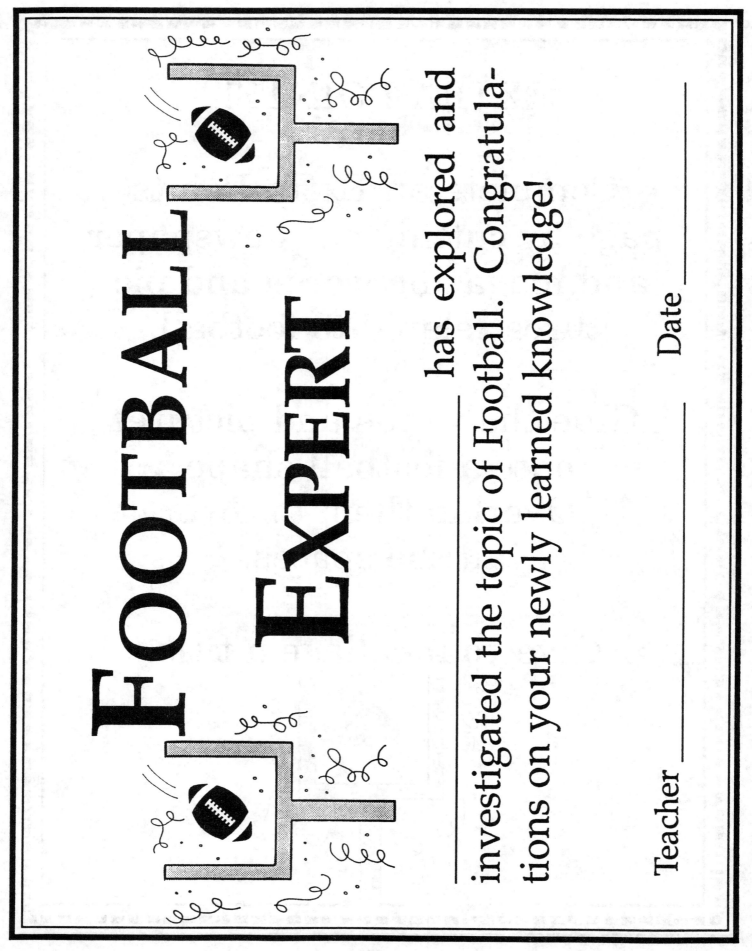

FOOTBALL EXPERT

_____ has explored and
investigated the topic of Football. Congratulations on your newly learned knowledge!

Teacher _____

Date _____

132

GA1393

THE MITTEN: A UKRAINIAN FOLKTALE

Jan Brett
G.P. Putnam's Sons, NY, 1990

A mitten becomes a home for a number of animals and a wonderful tale unfolds.

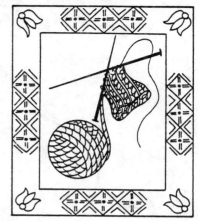

BLOOM'S QUESTIONS

KNOWLEDGE
Describe how the mitten house changed throughout the story.

COMPREHENSION
Explain all the reasons why the animals allowed the other animals to come into the mitten.

APPLICATION
If you had to ask one animal to leave, which one would it be and why?

ANALYSIS
Examine all the reasons a mitten might be a good house or a bad house for a mouse.

SYNTHESIS
Design a new house for the animals that would accommodate *all* the animals.

EVALUATION
Judge which one character might be the best roommate for the mouse.

CREATIVE THINKING ACTIVITIES

FLUENCY
Brainstorm a long list of as many kinds of winter clothing as you can.

FLEXIBILITY
Look at your list of clothing. Find an article of clothing that would make a good house for a mole, a rabbit, a hedgehog, an owl, a fox, a bear and a mouse.

*ORIGINALITY
The animals were not invited to Nicki's mitten, they just went in to escape the cold. Write an invitation from Nicki to the other animals *inviting* them to his mitten.

*ELABORATION
Look at the picture of Nicki's mitten in the story. Add details to the outside of the mitten to change its appearance.

GA1393

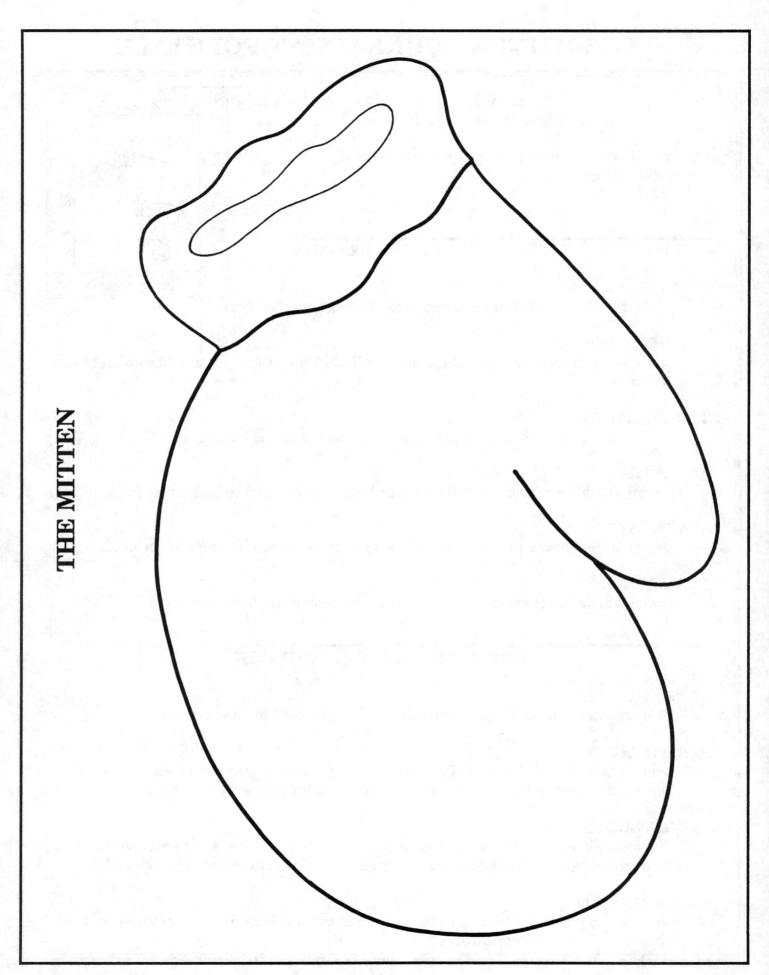

THE MITTEN

134

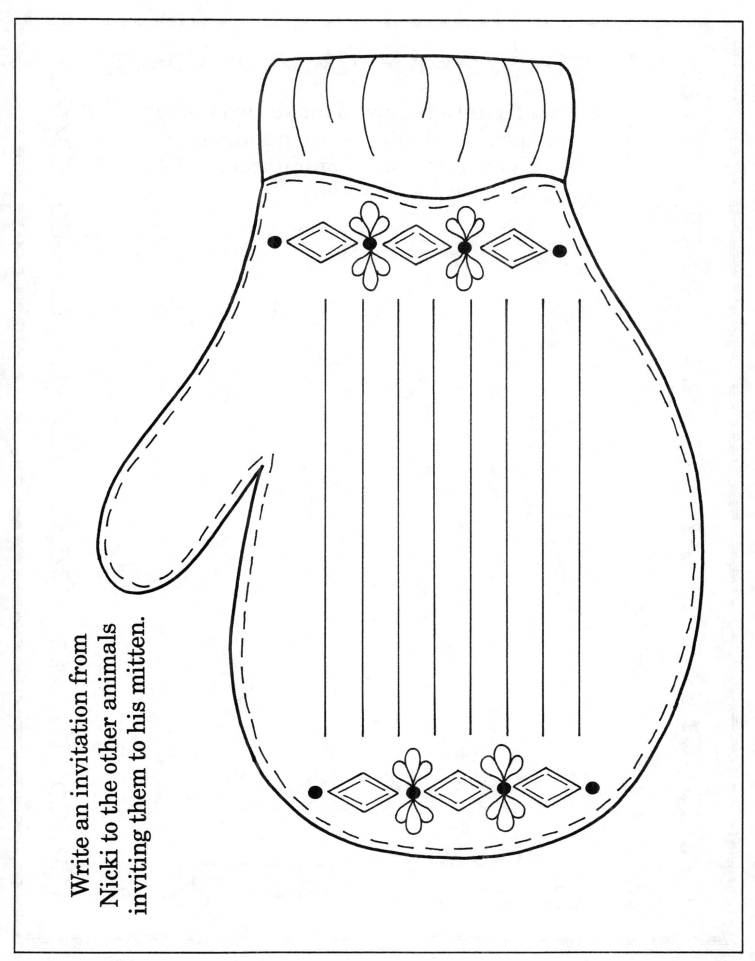

Write an invitation from
Nicki to the other animals
inviting them to his mitten.

135

Trace a friend's hands to make two mitten
shapes. Add interesting details to
make one-of-a-kind mittens.

Mitten Maker _____

136

GA1393

AMAZING ANIMALS RESEARCH

Research Project

+ Students will research at least seven facts about an animal of their choice.
+ Students will display their facts in a creative product of their choice.

Research Center

+ The Amazing Animals Research Center should include:

  • a special place in your classroom decorated with an animal theme, with items including cages, a safari hat, *Ranger Rick* and *My Big Backyard* magazines, stuffed animals and puppets related to wildlife.
  • animal research resources.
  • a laminated copy of the student activity packet (for teacher use and display at the center).

+ Provide each student with a copy of the animal notebook research shapes including the cover and student directions.

+ The completed research projects lend themselves well to holding a classroom Animal Fair. Other classrooms may visit and view the projects while asking student experts questions about their work.

+ Award each student an Expert Certificate upon completion of the center.

Research Resources

+ *Exotic Animals*. Dominguez Hills, CA: Educational Insights, 1990.

+ Felder, Deborah. *The Kids' World Almanac of Animals and Pets*. New York: Pharos Books, 1989.

+ Ganeri, Anita. *Animal Facts*. London: Usborne Publishing Co., 1988.

+ Sussman, Susan, and Robert James. *Lies (People Believe) About Animals*. Niles, Illinois: Albert Whitman & Co., 1987.

+ Venino, Susanne. *Amazing Animal Groups*. Washington, D.C.: National Geographic Society, 1981.

AMAZING ANIMALS RESEARCH

138

Select an animal of your choice or one of the animals in the book, *The Mitten*.

Read books about your animal to find the answers to the questions on the following pages.

Compile your information into a creative product such as a poster, diorama, puppet show, mobile or papier-mâché character.

What does the animal look like? Describe its color, special body parts, etc.

GA1393

Where does the animal live? Be specific.

GA1393

	What does the animal eat? How does it get its food?

What are the animal's enemies? How does the animal protect itself?

GA1393

How does the animal communicate with other animals?

GA1393

Other interesting facts.

GA1393

ANIMAL EXPERT

_____ has explored and investigated the topic of Animals. Congratulations on your newly learned knowledge!

Teacher _____

Date _____

146

GA1393

MUFARO'S BEAUTIFUL DAUGHTERS

John Steptoe
Scholastic, Inc., NY, 1987

Mufaro and his beautiful daughters journey to the city to meet the king, where a queen will be chosen.

BLOOM'S QUESTIONS

KNOWLEDGE
Who is Mufaro? Who is Manyara? Who is Nyasha?

COMPREHENSION
List five or more words to describe Manyara.

APPLICATION
Describe a time when your mother or father were proud of you. How did it make you feel?

ANALYSIS
Compare a modern-day wedding with Nyasha's wedding to Nyoka.

SYNTHESIS
Suppose Manyara had prevented Nyasha from meeting the king. How would the story have been different?

EVALUATION
Judge whether Nyoka's plan to determine who was the "most worthy and most beautiful daughter in the land" was a good one. Why or why not?

CREATIVE THINKING ACTIVITIES

FLUENCY
Make a long list of other stories that involve a king and a queen.

FLEXIBILITY
Look at your list above. Choose which king or queen you would most like to be.

*ORIGINALITY
Manyara was very greedy and anxious to become the queen. Fill out a complaint form about her behavior.

*ELABORATION
Elaborate on the white robes the characters wear. Add patterns, jewels, etc.

GA1393

MUFARO'S BEAUTIFUL DAUGHTERS

Manyara was very greedy and anxious to become queen. Fill out a complaint form about her behavior.

DATE:_____

TO:_____

FROM:_____

COMPLAINT:_____

_____

_____

_____

_____

_____

_____

_____

_____

_____

Elaborate on the plain white robes worn in the story.
Add details, patterns, jewels, etc.

Robe
Embellisher

ARTISTIC AFRICA RESEARCH

Research Project

✦ Students will research various types of African art.
✦ Students will create a picture replica of a piece of African art.

Research Center

✦ The Artistic Africa Research Center should include:

  • a special place in your classroom decorated with an African motif including African art prints, masks, native jewelry, fabric, pottery and baskets.
  • African art research resources.
  • a laminated copy of the student activity packet (for teacher use and display at the center).

✦ Provide each student with a copy of the African Art Masterpiece including the cover and student directions.

✦ The completed research project can be displayed on a bulletin board, easel or throughout the room as an African Art Gallery.

✦ Award each student an Expert Certificate upon completion of the center.

Research Resources

✦ Davidson, Marshall B. *A History of Art.* New York: Random House, 1984.

✦ Glubok, Shirley. *The Art of Africa.* New York: Harper & Row, 1965.

✦ Leuzinger, Elsy. *Africa.* New York: Crown Publishers, 1960.

✦ Read, Herbert. *Modern Sculpture.* New York: Praeger Publishers, 1974.

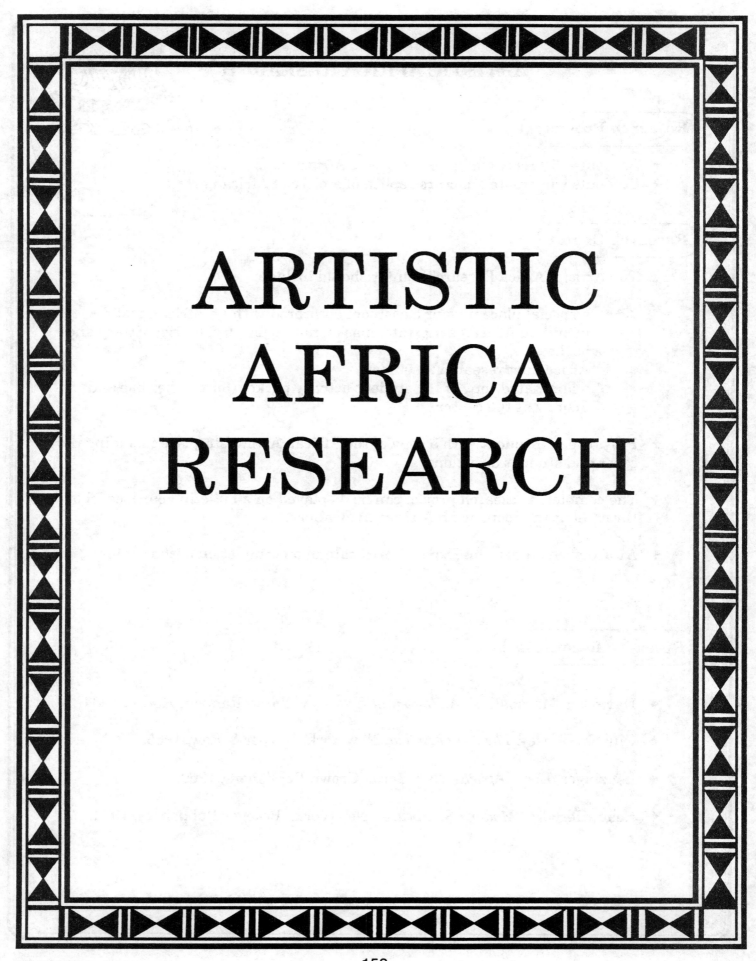

ARTISTIC AFRICA RESEARCH

152

Mufaro's Beautiful Daughters, by John Steptoe, is an African tale. The story takes place in an African country. Look closely at the illustrations in the book, especially the clothes, jewelry, pottery and baskets. Visit the library and find books about African Art. Select one piece of African Art and draw, color, paint or assemble a representation of it in the Masterpiece Frame provided. Label your picture with the name of the piece and the African country of its origin. Share any other interesting facts about your piece of artwork that you can find.

GA1393

African Masterpiece

GA1393

African Masterpiece Information

GA1393

AFRICAN ART EXPERT

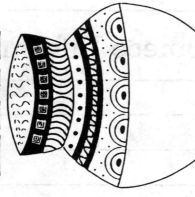

_____

has explored and investigated the topic of African Art. Congratulations on your newly learned knowledge!

Teacher _____

Date _____

156

THE QUILT STORY

Tony Johnston
Scholastic, Inc., NY, 1985

The Quilt Story follows two girls who share the same quilt and the security it provides.

BLOOM'S QUESTIONS

KNOWLEDGE
Describe Abigail's quilt.

COMPREHENSION
How did the quilt make Abigail feel better?

APPLICATION
Share something from your own life that makes you feel better when you are sad.

ANALYSIS
Compare Abigail's life with the other little girl's life in the story.

*SYNTHESIS
A mouse, raccoon and cat all loved Abigail's quilt. Design a special quilt for one of these animals to call its own.

EVALUATION
Debate whether it's a good idea to have a security object like Abigail's quilt.

CREATIVE THINKING ACTIVITIES

FLUENCY
With a friend, make a list of all the things you can think of that can become family heirlooms.

FLEXIBILITY
Think of a variety of uses for a quilt.

*ORIGINALITY
Create a recipe for comforting you when you are sad. Write it in recipe form.

ELABORATION
Elaborate on the meaning of the words: "So her mother rocked her as mothers do. Then tucked her in. And she felt at home again under the quilt."

THE QUILT STORY

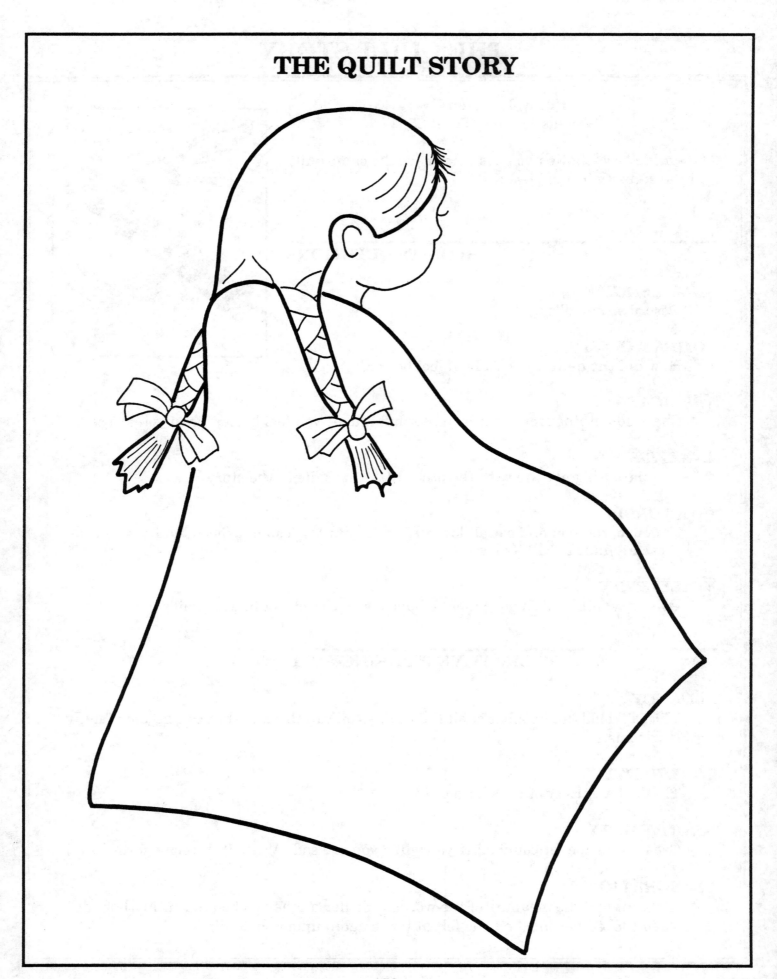

A mouse, raccoon
and cat all loved Abigail's quilt.
Design a special quilt for one
of these animals to call its own.

Quilt Designer _____

GA1393

Create a recipe for comforting you when you are sad. Write it in recipe form.

Comfort Recipe

Comfort Cook

GA1393

FAMILY HEIRLOOM RESEARCH

Research Project

✦ Students will interview adult family members as their resource guides.
✦ Students will create a family heirloom display.

Research Center

✦ The Family Heirloom Research Center should include:

  • a special place in your classroom decorated with family heirlooms or things that hold meaning to you and your students including quilts, books, teddy bears, photo albums, scrapbooks, etc.
  • heirloom research resources (you may want to include fiction books as well as resources of your own, such as a diary, journal or letters).
  • a laminated copy of the student activity packet (for teacher use and display at the center).

✦ Provide each student with a copy of the family heirloom interview sheet including the cover and student directions.

✦ The completed research projects can be displayed as a bulletin board, or set up as a museum display to be viewed by other classrooms.

✦ Award each student an Expert Certificate upon completion of the center.

Research Resources

✦ Atkins, Jacqueline. *Memories of Childhood.* New York: E.P. Dutton, 1989.

✦ Cooper, Patricia, and Norma Bradley Allen. *The Quilters.* New York: Doubleday, 1989.

✦ Rudstrom, Lennart. *A Home.* New York: G.P. Putnam's Sons, 1968.

✦ Smith, E. Boyd. *The Farm Book.* Boston: Houghton Mifflin Co., 1982.

✦ Tudor, Tasha. *Drawn From New England.* New York: Philomel Books, 1979.

FAMILY
HEIRLOOM
RESEARCH

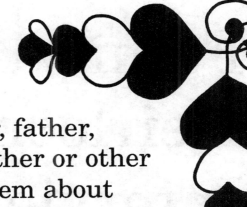

Interview your mother, father, grandmother, grandfather or other close relatives. Ask them about one of your family's heirlooms - maybe it is a quilt like Abigail's or a piece of jewelry or a favorite painting or book. Ask them about its history and why it is special to them.

Take notes on the interview form while you are listening to the information being shared. Draw a picture of your family's special heirloom and write about it.

Mount your picture and paragraph on a piece of poster board. Display it in your classroom. It will be interesting to read about each other's family heirlooms!

GA1393

Family Heirloom Interview

_____

_____

_____

_____

_____

_____

_____

_____

_____

_____

_____

_____

GA1393

Family Heirloom
Poster Layout

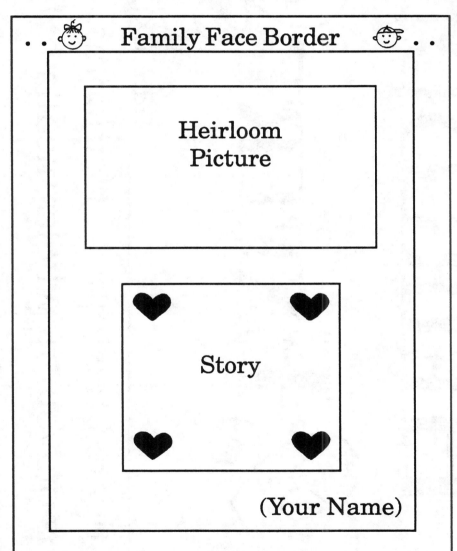

Family Face Border

Heirloom
Picture

Story

(Your Name)

165

GA1393

HEIRLOOM

EXPERT

_____ has explored and investigated the topic of Heirlooms. Congratulations on your newly learned knowledge!

Teacher _____

Date _____

ROSIE'S WALK

Pat Hutchins
Scholastic Inc., NY, 1968

Rosie, the hen, goes for a walk and sees many things in the farmyard.

BLOOM'S QUESTIONS

KNOWLEDGE
List three places the hen visited on her walk.

*COMPREHENSION
Draw a map showing each place Rosie went on her walk.

APPLICATION
If you went on a walk in a farmyard, what would you like to see?

ANALYSIS
How is Rosie like the fox? How is Rosie different from the fox?

SYNTHESIS
As a class, draw pictures of Rosie in a series of adventures in a new setting. Label each stop on Rosie's new walk and show what happens to the fox each time. Display the pictures in sequence on a mural.

EVALUATION
Judge which stop on the walk was least safe for Rosie.

CREATIVE THINKING ACTIVITIES

FLUENCY
List all the places you can think of that a hen can walk but a person cannot.

*FLEXIBILITY
Think of a new use for Rosie's chicken coop while she's out on her walk.

ORIGINALITY
Create a booklet of places to walk in your town. Send your completed book to your Chamber of Commerce.

ELABORATION
Elaborate on the relationship between the fox and the hen.

GA1393

ROSIE'S WALK

Draw a map showing each place
Rosie went on her walk.

Cartographer _____

GA1393

Think of a new use for Rosie's chicken coop while she's out on her walk.

Flexible Thinker _____

MAPPING YOUR WAY THROUGH RESEARCH

Research Project

- ✦ Students will research six facts on maps and globes.
- ✦ Students will create a maps and globes booklet.

Research Center

- ✦ The Mapping Your Way Through Research Center should include:

  - • a special place in your classroom decorated with a maps and globes theme including road maps, a globe, atlases, tour books and a compass.
  - • maps and globes research resources.
  - • a laminated copy of the student activity packet (for teacher use and display at the center).

- ✦ Provide each student with a copy of the maps and globes activity packet including the cover and student directions.

- ✦ The completed research project can be displayed as individual student booklets or as long map murals in scroll form.

- ✦ Award each student an Expert Certificate upon completion of the center.

Research Resources

- ✦ Knowlton, Jack. *Maps and Globes*. New York: Harper & Row, 1986.

- ✦ Roebuck, Wendy. *The Doubleday Picture Atlas*. New York: Doubleday, 1988.

- ✦ Tivers, Jacqueline, and Michael Day. *Children's World Atlas*. New York: The Viking Press, 1983.

- ✦ Wright, David, and Jill. *The Facts on File Children's Atlas*. New York: Facts on File, 1987.

- ✦ Tudor, Tasha. *Drawn From New England*. New York: Philomel Books, 1979.

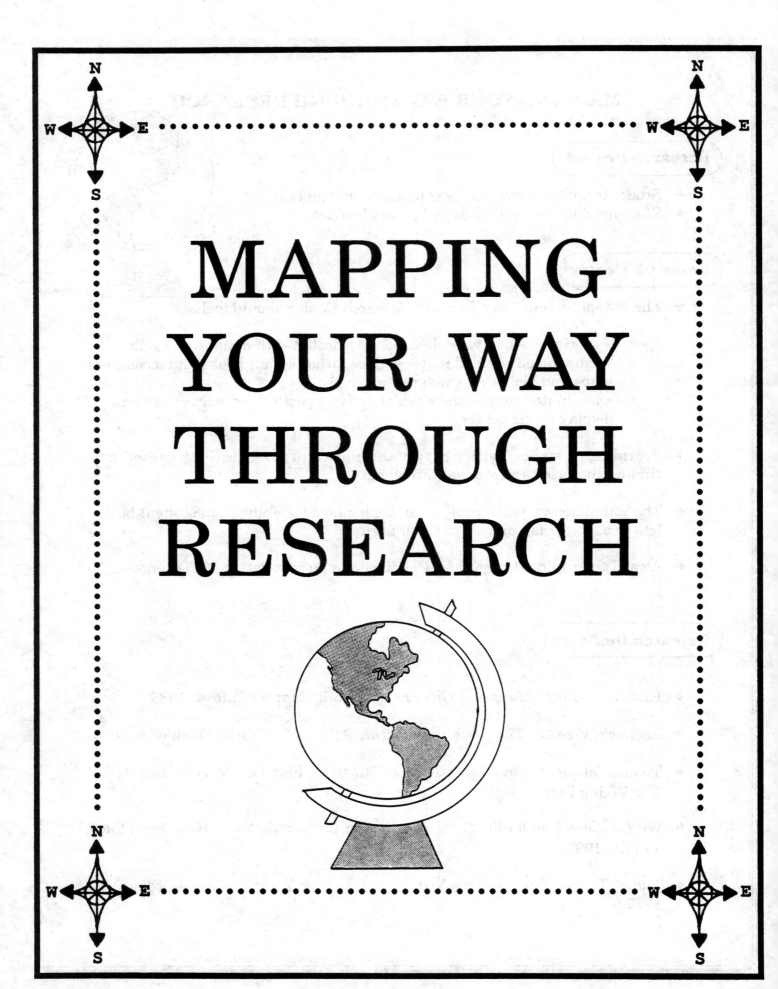

MAPPING YOUR WAY THROUGH RESEARCH

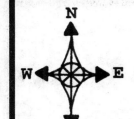

Read *Maps and Globes*, by Jack Knowlton.

Answer the questions on each scroll map.

Underline the word in each of your sentences that is directly related to maps and globes.

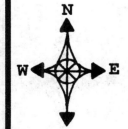
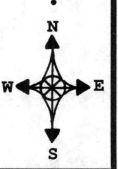

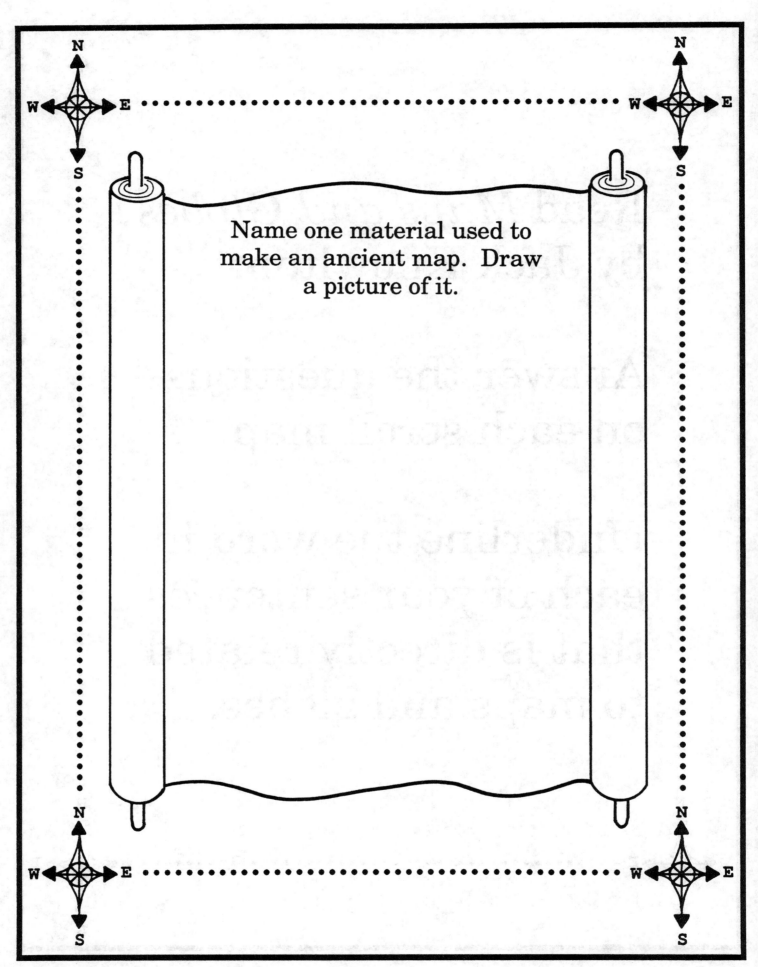

Name one material used to
make an ancient map. Draw
a picture of it.

174

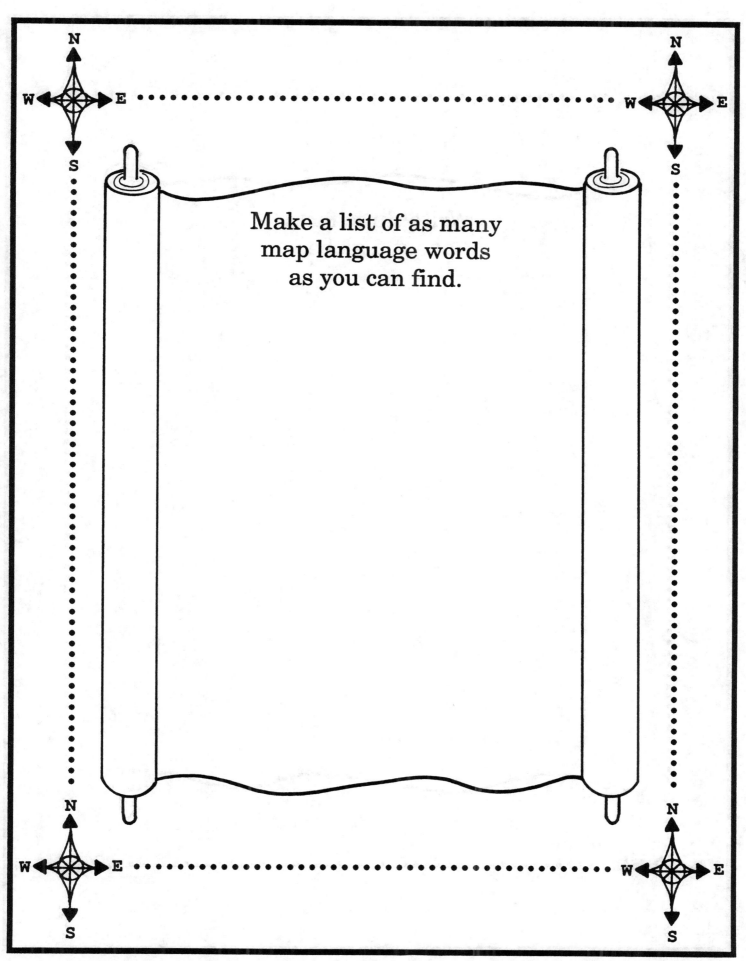

Make a list of as many
map language words
as you can find.

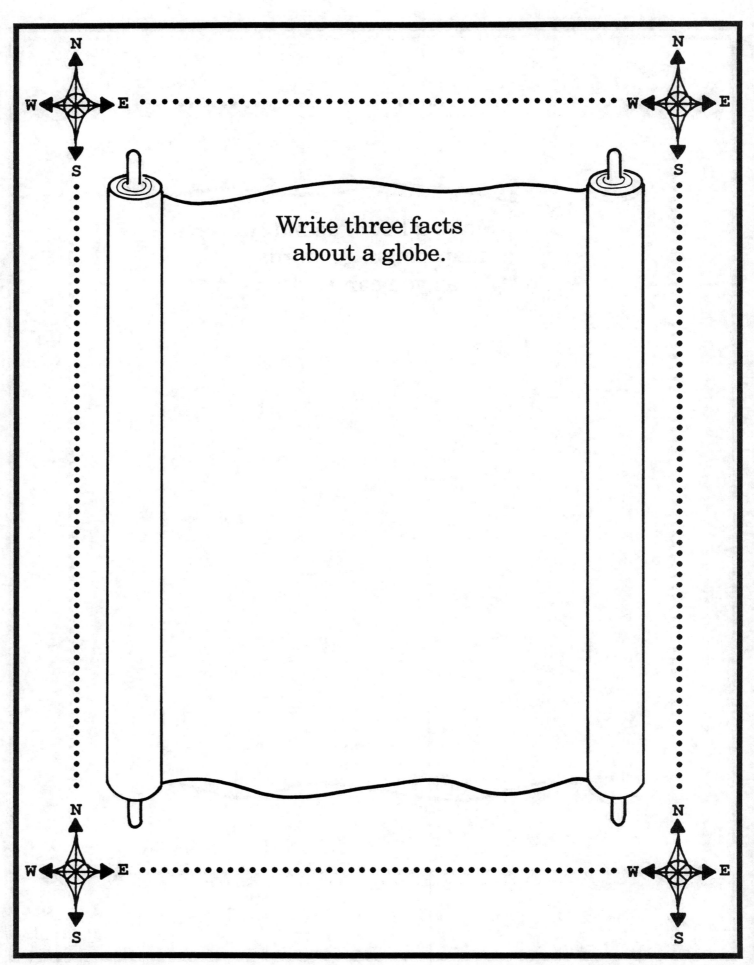

Write three facts
about a globe.

176

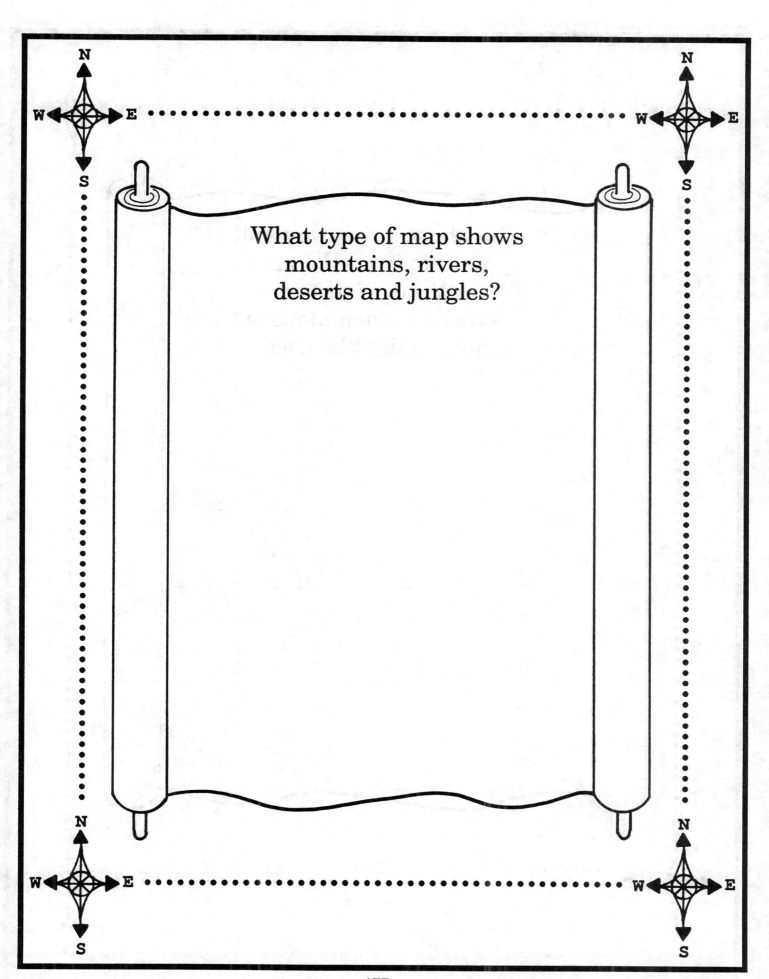

What type of map shows
mountains, rivers,
deserts and jungles?

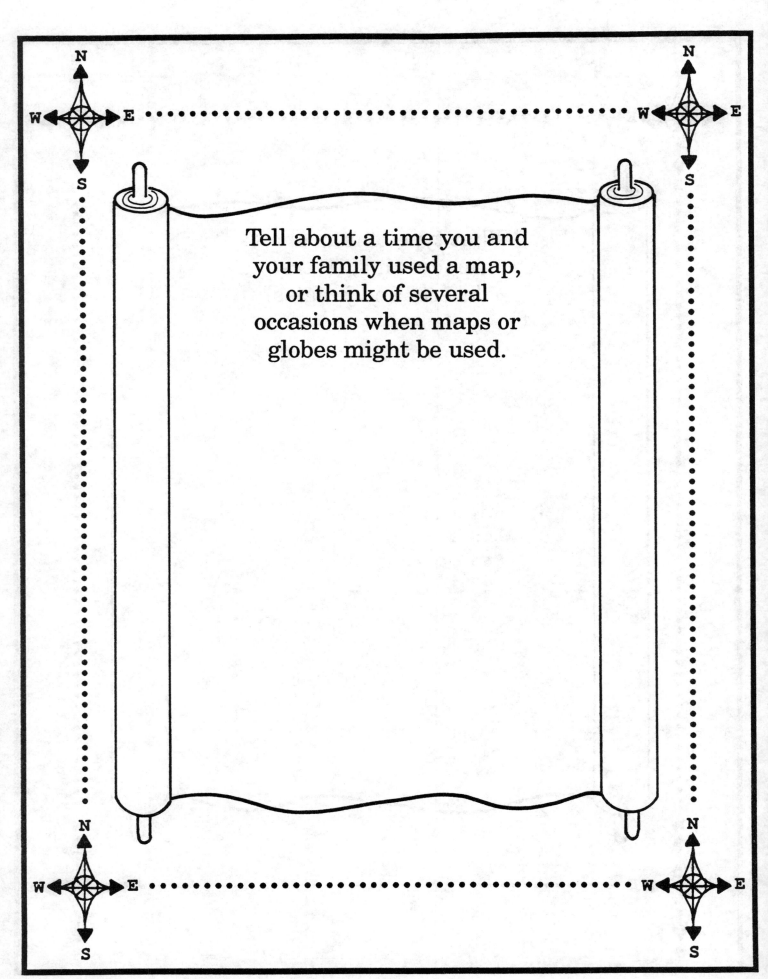

Tell about a time you and
your family used a map,
or think of several
occasions when maps or
globes might be used.

178

Now try your luck designing a map of your favorite room in your house. Use a large piece of paper. Be sure to include a key with map symbols.

KEY

Cut and paste on your map.

GA1393

MAP EXPERT

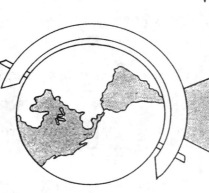

_____ has explored and
investigated the topic of Maps. Congratulations
on your newly learned knowledge!

Teacher _____

Date _____

GA1393

SAM, BANGS, & MOONSHINE

Evaline Ness
Trumpet Club, NY, 1966

The story of Sam, Thomas, & Bangs the cat, brings near disaster and a warm ending to the reader's heart.

BLOOM'S QUESTIONS

KNOWLEDGE
Share one or two of Sam's make-believe stories.

COMPREHENSION
What does the author mean by *moonshine* in the story?

APPLICATION
Share an example of *moonshine* from your own life.

ANALYSIS
Explain the difference between reality and *moonshine* and give examples of each.

*SYNTHESIS
Create a daydream you would like to have. Draw a picture of it.

EVALUATION
Was Sam's *moonshine* a good idea? Why or why not?

CREATIVE THINKING ACTIVITIES

FLUENCY
Brainstorm actions that deserve an apology.

*FLEXIBILITY
Sam apologized to Thomas by giving him the gerbil. Draw a picture of another way Sam might have apologized to Thomas.

ORIGINALITY
Design a special home for Bangs. Make it a home a cat would love.

ELABORATION
Read the last page of the story and elaborate on the conversation between Thomas and Sam. What else did they say to each other?

GA1393

GA1393

Illustrate a daydream you would like to have.

Daydreamer _____

GA1393

SORRY – SORRY – SORRY – SORRY – SORRY – SORRY – SORRY – SORRY

Draw a picture of another way Sam might have apologized to Thomas.

Apology Giver _____

SORRY – SORRY – SORRY – SORRY – SORRY – SORRY – SORRY – SORRY

SORRY – SORRY – SORRY – SORRY – SORRY – SORRY – SORRY – SORRY

184

GA1393

THE CAT'S MEOW RESEARCH

Research Project

✦ Students will research seven cat facts.
✦ Students will create a Cat Shape Book.

Research Center

✦ The Cat's Meow Research Center should include:

- a special place in your classroom decorated with a cat theme including stuffed cats, a cat basket, a cat dish and cat toys.
- cat research resources.
- a laminated copy of the student activity packet (for teacher use and display at the center).

✦ Provide each student with a copy of the cat research shapes including the cover and student directions.

✦ The completed research project can be displayed as individual cat shape books or as a cat collage poster with magazine pictures added.

✦ Award each student an Expert Certificate upon completion of the center.

Research Resources

✦ Calder, S.J. *If You Were a Cat*. Englewood Cliffs, N.J.: Silver Press, 1989.

✦ Eisler, Colin. *Cats Know Best*. New York: Dial Books, 1988.

✦ Hill, Rose. *Cats and Kittens*. London: Usborne Publishing Co., 1982.

✦ Kunhardt, Edith. *Kittens, Kittens, Kittens*. New York: A Golden Book, 1987.

✦ Lewis, Sharon. *Tigers*. New York: Harper & Row, 1990.

GA1393

THE CAT'S MEOW RESEARCH

GA1393

Write a fun cat title
and your name on the
first cat shape.

Then complete each
cat fact using books from
the library. Add colorful
details around your words
to give each cat a unique
personality.

Cut out each cat and
assemble into a cat book.

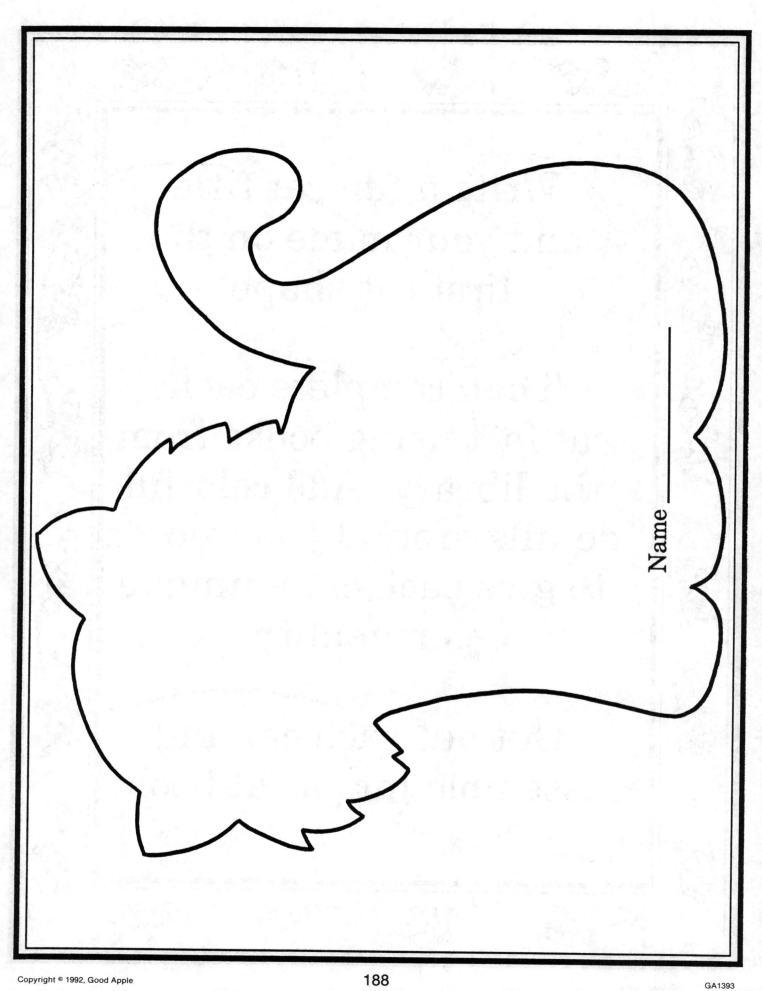

Name _____

188

GA1393

Members of the cat family . . .

189

Where cats live . . . .

190

What cats look like . . .

GA1393

Things cats like . . .

192

Things cats dislike . . .

193

Words that rhyme with cat . . . .

194

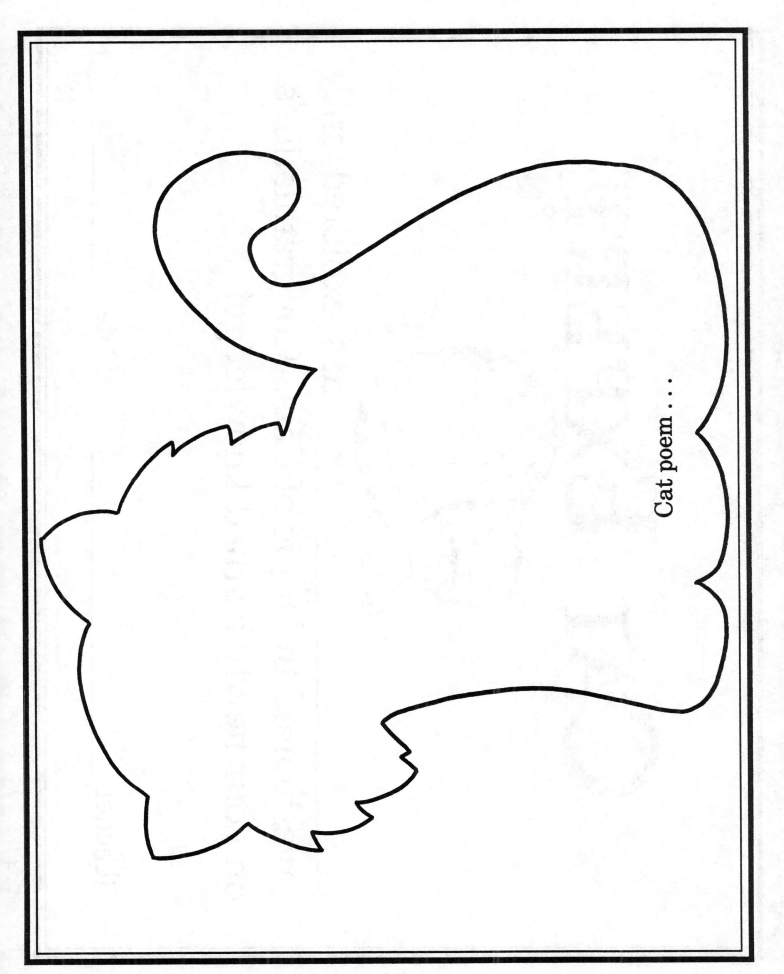

Cat poem . . . .

Cat Expert

_____ has explored and
investigated the topic of Cats. Congratulations
on your newly learned knowledge!

Teacher _____

Date _____

THERE'S A NIGHTMARE IN MY CLOSET

Mercer Mayer
Weekly Reader Press, NY, 1968

A little boy explains his solution to getting rid of a nightmare in his closet.

BLOOM'S QUESTIONS

KNOWLEDGE
What was the little boy afraid of?

COMPREHENSION
Why was the little boy afraid of the Nightmare?

APPLICATION
What do *you* do to make a nightmare disappear?

ANALYSIS
Compare the Nightmare in the book with a nightmare in your own life.

SYNTHESIS
Look at each page showing the Nightmare. The Nightmare never talks. Tell what you think the Nightmare might be saying or thinking on each page.

EVALUATION
Was the little boy's solution to make the Nightmare go away a good one? Why?

CREATIVE THINKING ACTIVITIES

FLUENCY
Brainstorm a list of frightening things.

FLEXIBILITY
Categorize the list of frightening things. Select the *most* frightening thing from your list.

*ORIGINALITY
Invent a new solution to get rid of a nightmare or frightening thing. Draw a picture of your solution and describe how it works.

*ELABORATION
Add details/decorations to the little boy's closet door in the story. (Display the finished doors on your classroom door.)

GA1393

THERE'S A NIGHTMARE IN MY CLOSET

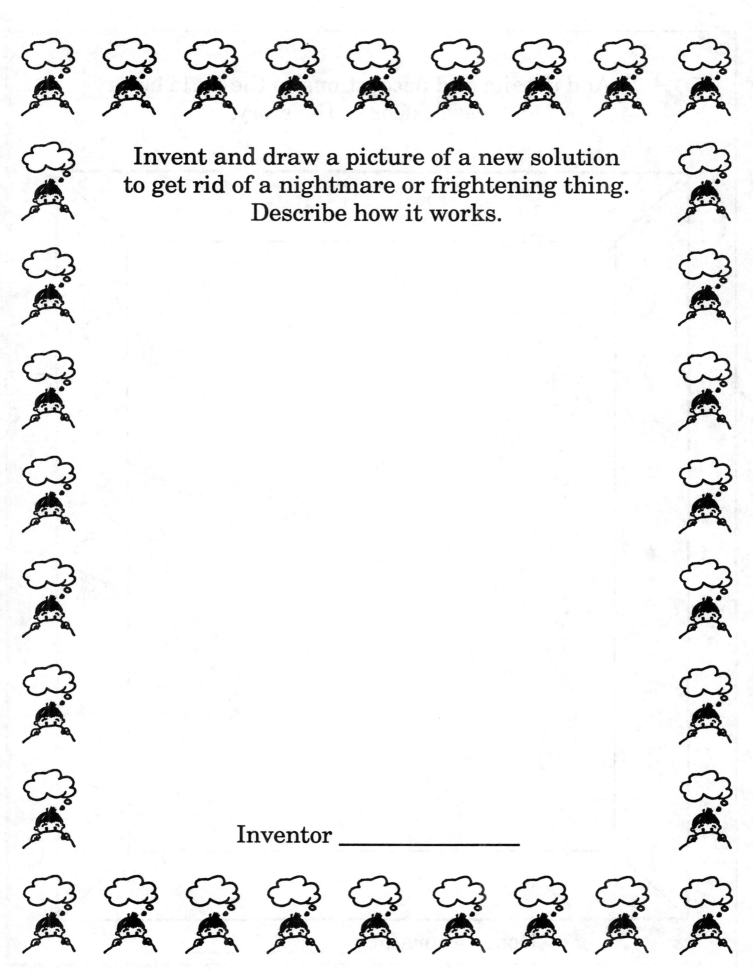

Invent and draw a picture of a new solution
to get rid of a nightmare or frightening thing.
Describe how it works.

Inventor _____

GA1393

Add details and decorations to the little boy's closet door in the story.

Door Decorator _____

MIDNIGHT CREATURES RESEARCH

Research Project

+ ◆ Students will research interesting facts on a midnight animal of their choice.
+ ◆ Students will create a picture and paragraph about their creature.

Research Center

+ ◆ The Midnight Creatures Research Center should include:

  • a special place in your classroom decorated with a midnight animal theme including pictures of midnight animals, a flashlight, an animal cage and binoculars.
  • night creatures research resources.
  • a laminated copy of the student activity packet (for teacher use and display at the center).

+ ◆ Provide each student with a copy of the creature research form including the cover and student directions.

+ ◆ The completed research project can be displayed in poster form or as a class-book or as a hallway display.

+ ◆ Award each student an Expert Certificate upon completion of the center.

Research Resources

+ ◆ Bason, Lillian. *Spiders*. Washington, D.C.: National Geographic, 1974.

+ ◆ Cole, Joanna. *A Snake's Body*. New York: Morrow, 1981.

+ ◆ Cutts, David. *I Can Read About Creatures of the Night*. New York: Troll Associates, 1979.

+ ◆ Kostyal, K.M. *Raccoons*. Washington, D.C.: National Geographic, 1987.

+ ◆ Tunney, Christopher. *Midnight Animals*. New York: Random House, 1987.

MIDNIGHT CREATURES RESEARCH

GA1393

The Nightmare in the closet only appeared when the little boy went to bed and the room was dark. The Nightmare could be called a "Midnight Creature." Did you know that there are real creatures of the night? For example, fireflies, moths, bats, desert mice, owls and porcupines all wake up when the sun goes down.

Select a creature of the night from the list above or one of your own choice and read about it. Then draw a picture of your creature and write a short description of it. Be sure to include a fascinating fact about your creature.

GA1393

Meet A
Midnight Creature

_____

GA1393

Read About A Midnight Creature

GA1393

MIDNIGHT CREATURE EXPERT

_____ has explored and investigated the topic of Midnight Creatures. Congratulations on your newly learned knowledge!

Teacher _____

Date _____

WHAT THE MAILMAN BROUGHT

Carolyn Craven
G.P. Putnam's Sons, NY, 1987

Five unusual mailmen deliver a variety of packages to William, who is home sick from school.

BLOOM'S QUESTIONS

KNOWLEDGE
List five unusual mailmen found in the book.

COMPREHENSION
What is the connection between the mailmen and the packages delivered to William?

APPLICATION
Draw a picture of your favorite scene from your bedroom window.

ANALYSIS
How are the mailmen in the story alike? How are they different?

SYNTHESIS
With a friend, discuss a new ending for the story and share it with the class.

EVALUATION
Debate whether William was imagining the mailmen or not.

CREATIVE THINKING ACTIVITIES

FLUENCY
List as many cures for boredom as you can.

FLEXIBILITY
Select your favorite cure for boredom and tell why it works.

*ORIGINALITY
Draw a picture of your own unusual mail carrier and the gift he or she would bring.

*ELABORATION
Discuss how and why William knew the mailman would not return at the end of the story.

GA1393

WHAT THE MAILMAN BROUGHT

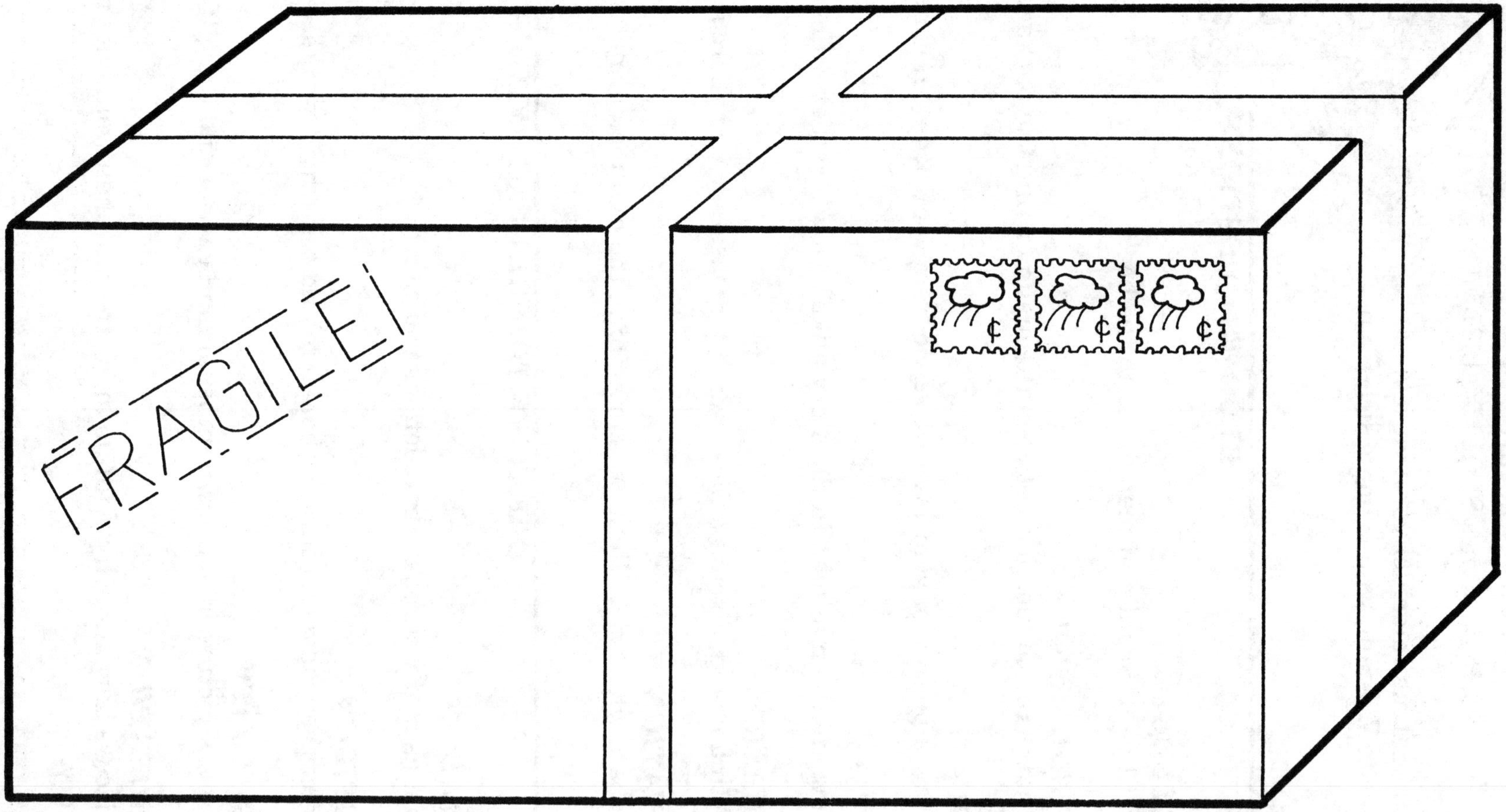

FRAGILE!

GA1393

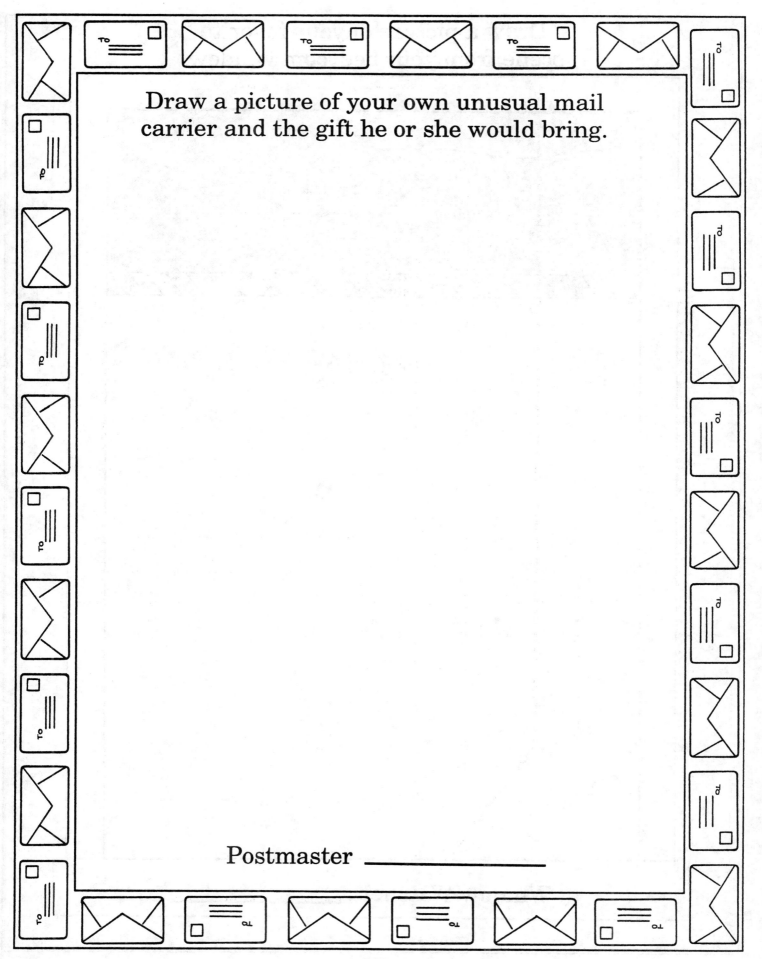

Draw a picture of your own unusual mail carrier and the gift he or she would bring.

Postmaster _____

Draw a picture of your favorite scene from your bedroom window.

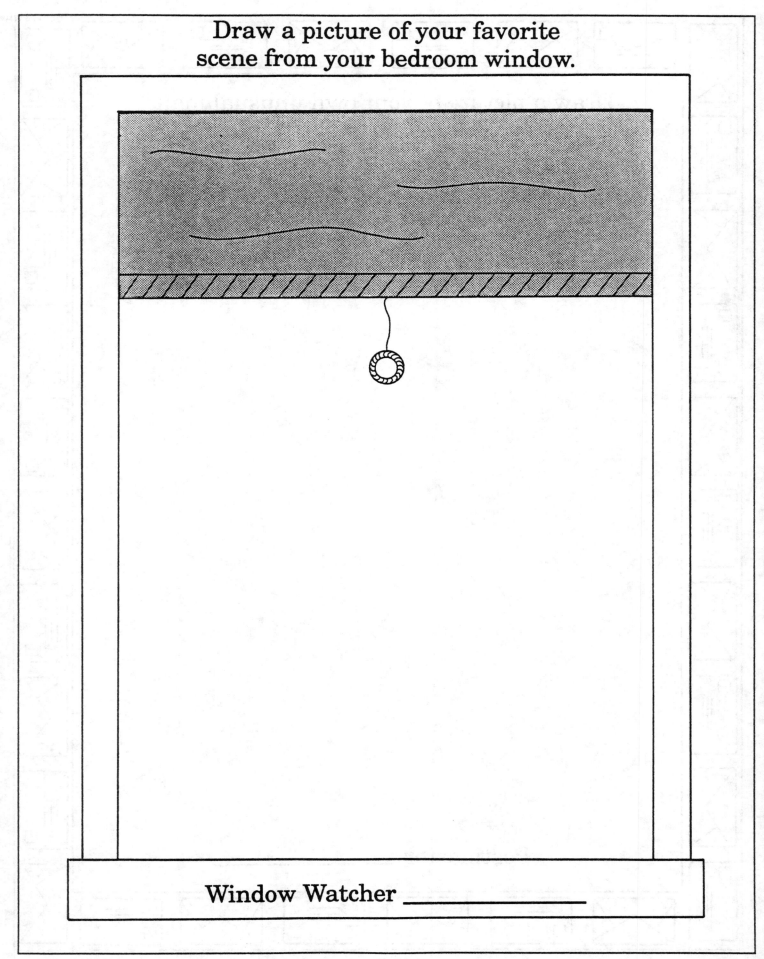

Window Watcher _____

STAMP INTO RESEARCH

Research Project

✦ Students will research seven facts about the Post Office.
✦ Students will create a stamp mobile or booklet.

Research Center

✦ The Stamp into Research Center should include:

  • a special place in your classroom decorated with a postal theme including a toy mailbox, envelopes, stationery, mailbag, etc.
  • post office research resources.
  • a laminated copy of the student activity packet (for teacher use and display at the center).

✦ Provide each student with a copy of the postage stamp research shapes including the cover and student directions.

✦ The completed research project can be displayed as mobiles or as individual booklets. Take the finished products to your local post office for public display.

✦ Award each student an Expert Certificate upon completion of the center.

Research Resources

✦ Gibbons, Gail. *The Post Office Book: Mail and How It Works.* New York: Harper Trophy, 1986.

✦ Johnson, Jean. *Postal Workers A-Z.* New York: Walker & Co., 1987.

✦ Matthews, Morgan. *What's It Like to Be a Postal Worker.* New York: Troll Associates, 1989.

✦ Ziegler, Sandra. *A Visit to the Post Office.* New York: Children's Press, 1989.

✦ See your local Postmaster for more information.

GA1393

STAMP INTO RESEARCH

GA1393

Read *The Post Office Book*, by Gail Gibbons.

Complete each postage stamp using complete sentences and assemble as a mobile.

Be sure to decorate the unwritten side of each stamp.

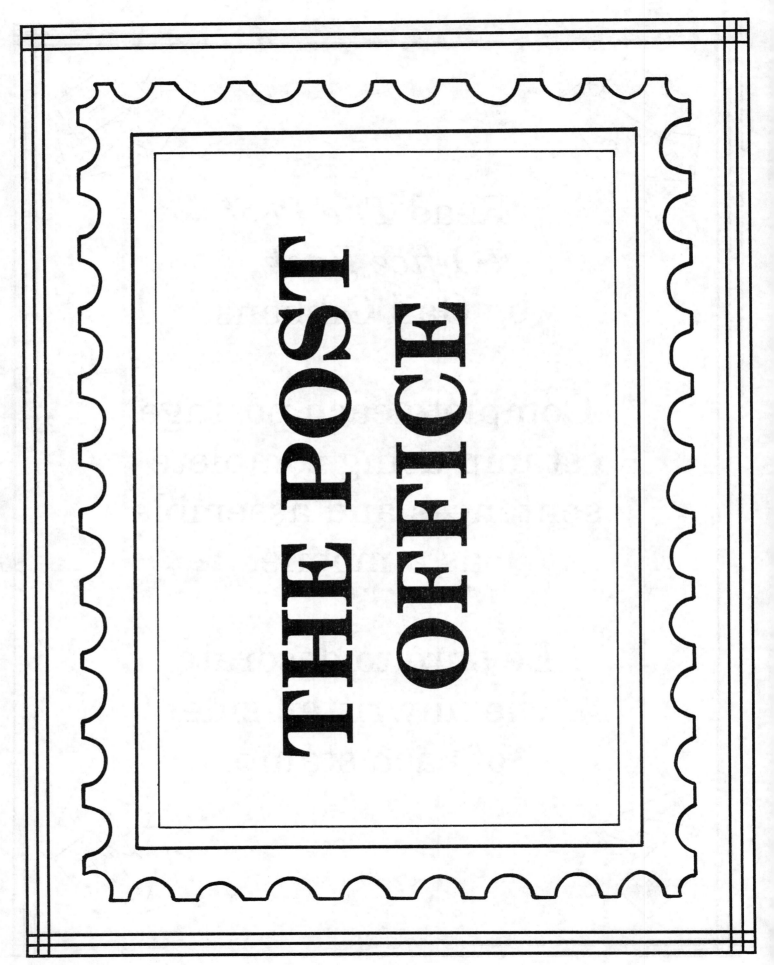

THE POST OFFICE

214

Draw a picture of one way mail was delivered in earlier days.

GA1393

Explain the job of a cancelling machine.

216

Tell how the price of each letter is determined.

Where is oversized or odd-shaped
mail placed at the post office?

Write the zip code for your town.

GA1393

Write your own mailing address.

What is the address of a post office in your town?

GA1393

Post Office Expert

_____ has explored and investigated the topic of Post Offices. Congratulations on your newly learned knowledge!

Teacher _____

Date _____

THE YEAR OF THE PERFECT CHRISTMAS TREE

Gloria Houston
Dial Books, NY, 1988

A timeless story about a family's power and courage during
the Christmas season.

BLOOM'S QUESTIONS

KNOWLEDGE
Describe Ruthie. Describe Mama.

COMPREHENSION
Why was it important that Ruthie "mark the Christmas tree"?

APPLICATION
Share a special time in your life similar to Ruthie's selection as the heavenly angel.

ANALYSIS
Compare Ruthie's Christmas to your own Christmas. How is it similar? How is it
different?

SYNTHESIS
How else could Ruthie and her Mama have taken the Christmas tree from the mountain?

EVALUATION
Share three things the story teaches you. Tell why.

CREATIVE THINKING ACTIVITIES

FLUENCY
Create a long list of Christmas traditions.

*FLEXIBILITY
Think of different uses for a Christmas tree beginning December 26.

*ORIGINALITY
Choosing a theme, decorate a one-of-a-kind Christmas tree. Make it as unusual as
you can.

ELABORATION
Elaborate on the last line of the story: "Grandma Ruthie told me so."

GA1393

GA1393

Think of different uses for a Christmas tree beginning December 26. Illustrate your most unique idea.

Tree Recycler _____

Choose a theme: Decorate a one-of-a-kind
Christmas tree using your theme.
Make it as unusual as you can.

Tree Designer _____

GA1393

OH, CHRISTMAS TREE RESEARCH

Research Project

✦ Students will research nine Christmas tree facts.
✦ Students will create a Christmas tree shape book.

Research Center

✦ The Oh, Christmas Tree Research Center should include:

- a special place in your classroom decorated with a Christmas motif including an artificial Christmas tree, unusual decorations, and attractive Christmas gift bags to keep books and materials.
- Christmas tree and/or tree research resources.
- a laminated copy of the student activity packet (for teacher use and display at the center).

✦ Provide each student with a set of Christmas tree research shapes including the cover and student directions.

✦ The completed research project can be displayed as individual shape books, a class mural on Christmas wrapping paper or as student posters.

✦ Award each student an Expert Certificate upon completion of the center.

Research Resources

✦ Braithwaite, Althea. *Tree*. London: Longman, 1982.

✦ Brandt, Keith. *Discovery Trees*. Mahwah, New Jersey: Troll Associates, 1982.

✦ Burnie, David. *Tree*. New York: Alfred A. Knopf, 1989.

✦ Dickinson, Jane. *All About Trees*. Mahwah, New Jersey: Troll Associates, 1989.

✦ Henderson, Kathy. *Christmas Trees*. Chicago: Children's Press, 1989.

✦ Martin, Alexander C., and Herbert S. Zim. *Trees*. New York: Golden Press, 1987.

OH, CHRISTMAS TREE RESEARCH

Find a book about trees in the library.

Write the title, Christmas Trees, and your name on the first tree shape. Add details to make a beautiful cover.

Then complete each tree fact. Write your fact in a whole sentence on the shape. Cut out and decorate each tree and assemble as a book.

229

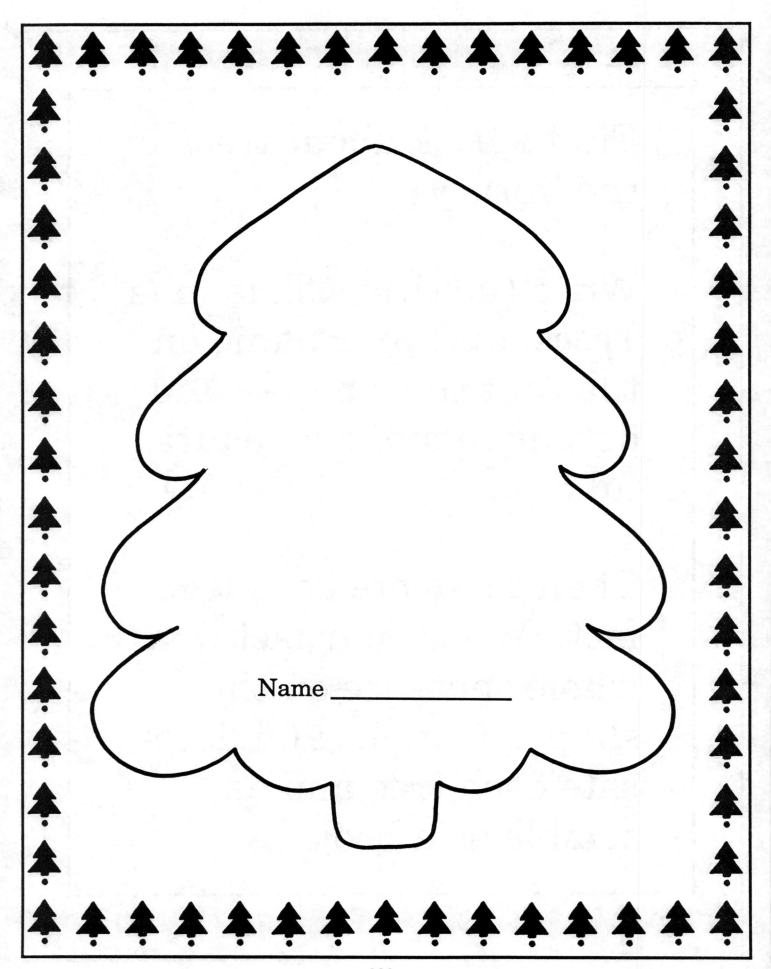

Name _____

230

Write the name of three different
types of Christmas trees.

231

List three places in the United States
where Christmas trees are grown.

Select one type of Christmas tree and
share a unique fact about it.

233

Draw a picture of your favorite type
of Christmas tree.

234

GA1393

Draw a picture of one type of
pinecone. Label your picture.

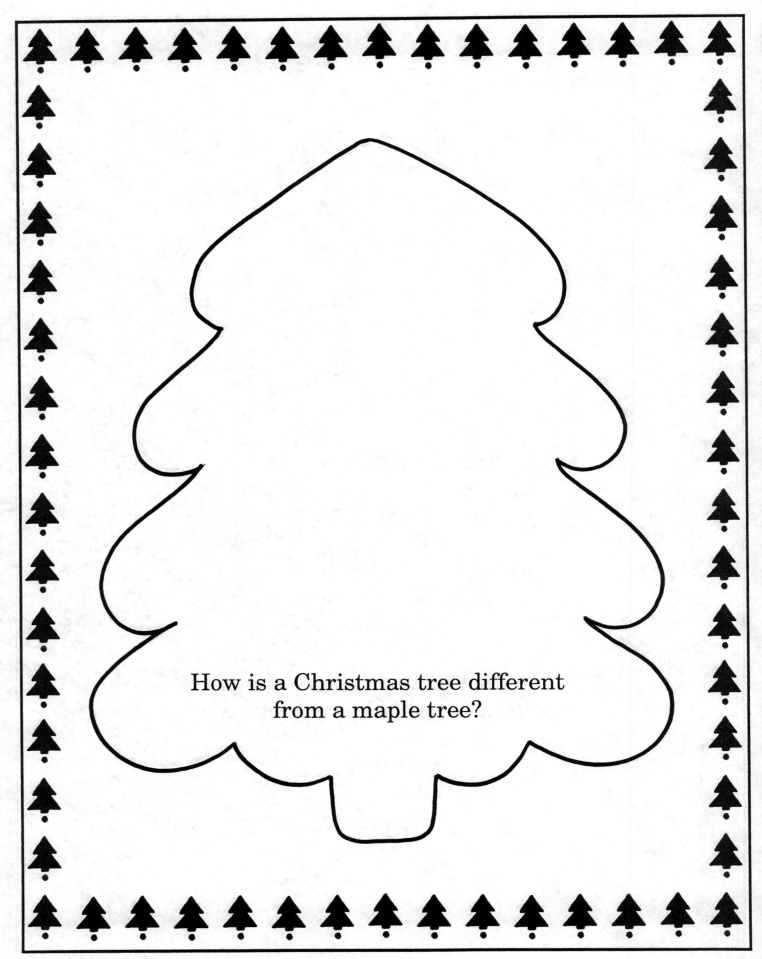

How is a Christmas tree different
from a maple tree?

236

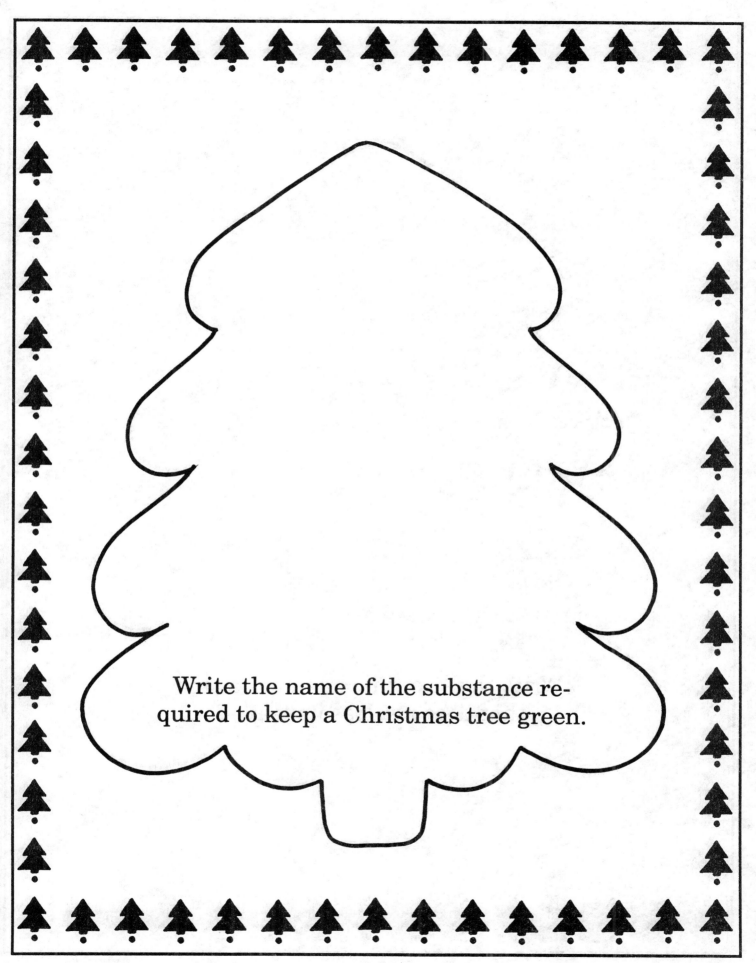

Write the name of the substance required to keep a Christmas tree green.

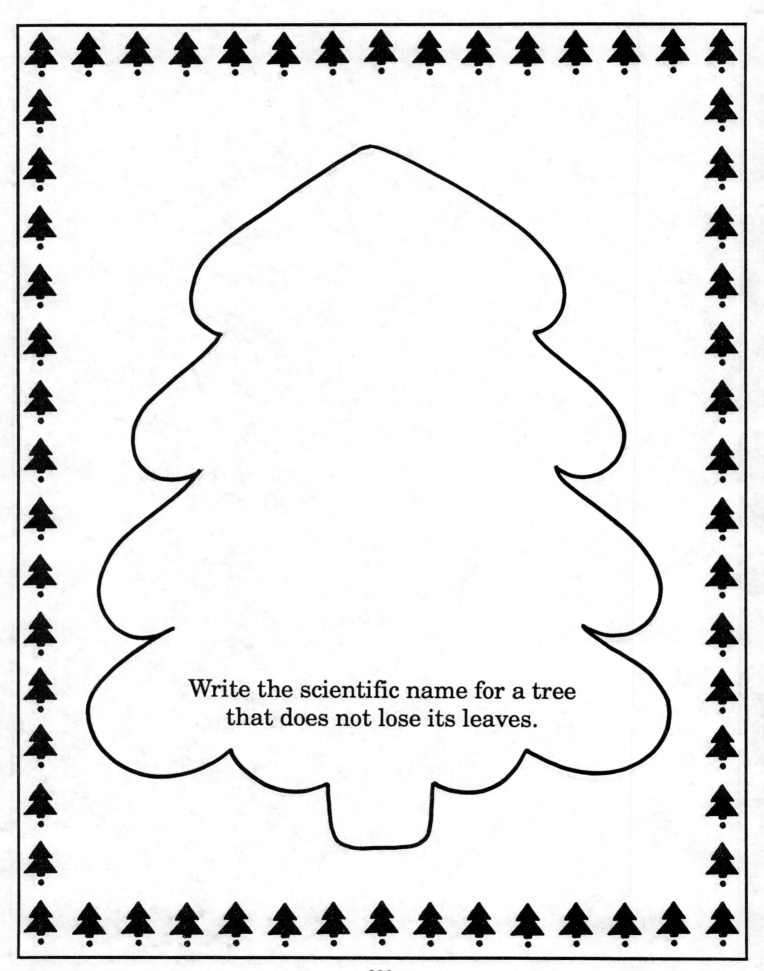

Write the scientific name for a tree
that does not lose its leaves.

238

GA1393

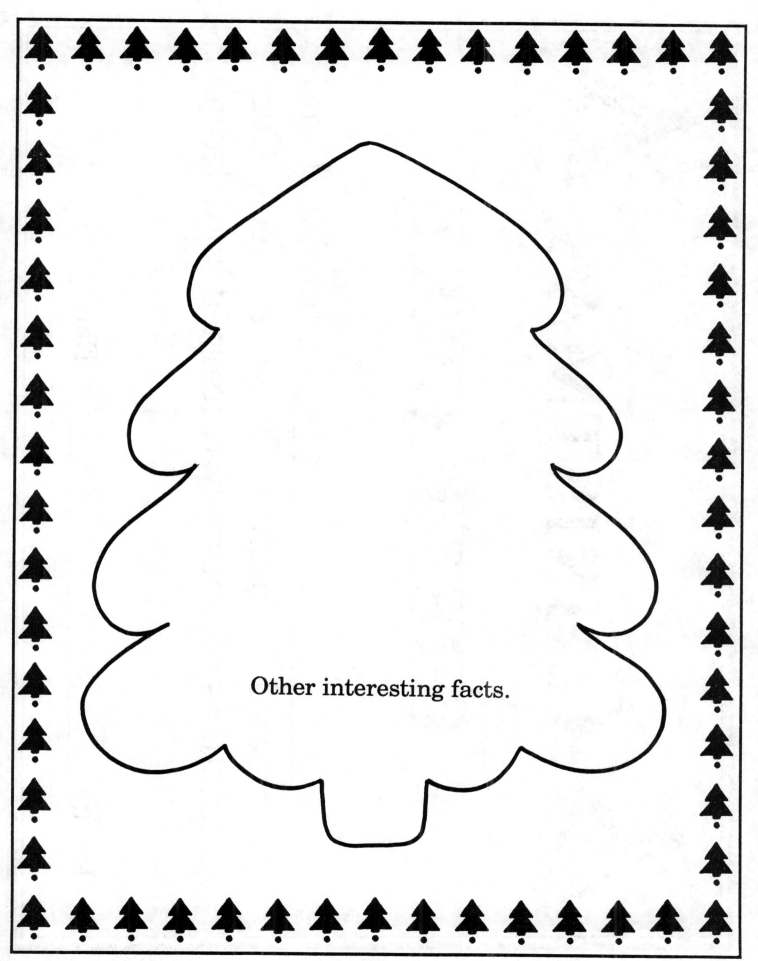

Other interesting facts.

239

CHRISTMAS TREE EXPERT

_____

has explored and investigated the topic of Christmas Trees. Congratulations on your newly learned knowledge!

Teacher _____

Date _____

GA1393

Bibliography

Allard, Harry, and James Marshall. *Miss Nelson Has a Field Day*. Boston: Houghton Mifflin Co., 1985.

Bemelmans, Ludwig. *Madeline*. New York: Scholastic, Inc., 1939.

Brett, Jan. *The Mitten: A Ukrainian Folktale*. New York: G.P. Putnam's Sons, 1990.

Burton, Virginia Lee. *Katy and the Big Snow*. New York: Scholastic, Inc., 1943.

Carle, Eric. *The Grouchy Ladybug*. New York: Thomas Y. Crowell, 1977.

Carle, Eric. *A House for Hermit Crab*. New York: Picture Book Studios, 1987.

Craven, Carolyn. *What the Mailman Brought*. New York: G.P. Putnam's Sons, 1987.

Dr. Seuss. *Horton Hatches the Egg*. New York: Random House, Inc., 1940.

The Gingerbread Man. New York: Scholastic, Inc., 1967.

Hoban, Russell. *Bedtime for Frances*. New York: Scholastic, Inc., 1960.

Houston, Gloria. *The Year of the Perfect Christmas Tree*. New York: Dial Books, 1988.

Hutchins, Pat. *Rosie's Walk*. New York: Scholastic, Inc., 1968.

GA1393

Johnston, Tony. *The Quilt Story*. New York: Scholastic , Inc., 1985.

Mayer, Mercer. *There's a Nightmare in My Closet*. New York: Weekly Reader Press, 1968.

Ness, Evaline. *Sam, Bangs, & Moonshine*. New York: Trumpet Club, 1966.

Pinkwater, Daniel Manus. *The Big Orange Splot*. New York: Scholastic, Inc., 1977.

Steptoe, John. *Mufaro's Beautiful Daughters*. New York: Scholastic, Inc., 1987.

Ward, Lynd. *The Biggest Bear*. Boston: Houghton Mifflin Co., 1952.

GA1393